Life After Big Bang

Chairman and General Editor: Simon macLachlan,
Clifford Chance, London

Proceedings of an international seminar (Life After Big Bang) organised by the International Bar Association Section on Business Law and held in London, 14 September 1987.

Graham & Trotman
A member of the Kluwer Academic Publishers Group
LONDON/DORDRECHT/BOSTON

and

International Bar Association

First published in 1987 by
Graham & Trotman Limited
Sterling House
66 Wilton Road
London SW1V 1DE
UK

Graham & Trotman Inc.
Kluwer Academic Publishers Group
101 Philip Drive
Assinippi Park
Norwell, MA 02061
USA

International Bar Association
2 Harewood Place
Hanover Square
London W1R 9HB
UK

British Library Cataloguing in Publication Data
Life After Big Bang (1987; London)
Life after big bang: proceedings of an international seminar (Life After Big Bang).
1. Financial institutions — Great Britain
2. Financial institutions — Law and legislation — Great Britain
I. Title II. International Bar Association,
Section on Business Law
III. macLachlan, Simon
332.1'0941 HG186.G7

ISBN: 0-86010-982-8

Library of Congress Cataloguing-in-Publication Data is available.

ISBN: 0 86010 982 8

Printed and bound in Great Britain by the Alden Press, Oxford.

Contents

Throughout the Seminar questions and discussion were provided by a panel of commentators consisting of:
Peter Dey, Osler Hoskin & Harcourt, Toronto
Simon macLachlan, Clifford Chance, London
Leigh Masel, Phillips Fox, Melbourne
Noboru Nakagawa, Nakagawa Godo Law Office, Tokyo
Joni Nelson, Rogers & Wells, New York
Richard Nettleton, Mallesons Stephen Jaques, Sydney
André Newburg, Cleary Gottlieb Steen & Hamilton, New York
James Riley, Stikeman Elliott, Toronto
J. Michael Robinson QC, Faskin & Calvin, Toronto
Al Sommer, Morgan Lewis & Bockius, Washington
Dr. Hans Rudolf Steiner, Walder Wyss & Partners, Zurich

About the IBA and the Section on Business Law and its Committee on Issues and Trading in Securities

The International Bar Association is the world's foremost association of lawyers, with a membership of over 11,000 individual lawyers in 120 countries, as well as 104 Bar Associations and Law Societies. Its principal aims and objectives are:

To encourage the discussion of problems relating to professional organisation and status.
To promote an exchange of information between legal associations worldwide.
To support the independence of the judiciary and the right of lawyers to practise their profession without interference.
To keep abreast of developments in the law, and help in improving and making new laws.

Above all, though, it seeks to provide a forum in which individual lawyers can contact, and exchange ideas with, other lawyers.

The IBA has three sections of which the Section on Business Law (SBL) is the largest with approximately 8,200 members. The SBL was established to promote an interchange of information and views amongst members of the IBA as to laws, practices and procedures affecting business, financial and commercial activities throughout the world. The Section is divided into 24 specialist committees. The Committee on Issues and Trading in Securities has over 720 members.

The Committee deals with all aspects of securities' laws and regulations in various legal and market environments ranging from highly regulated to virtually unregulated. Rapidly changing laws and markets produce new subjects of interest regularly, thus providing a range of topics for discussion at the Committee's annual meeting. The Committee also organises a number of Seminars of which this is one.

One of the most important aims of the Committee, and one which has been most successfully accomplished, is to enable Committee members to become personally acquainted with qualified colleagues in other countries specialising in the same areas, to whom they may turn for professional assistance in their own international practice.

Further details of the IBA and SBL are available from: 2 Harewood Place, Hanover Square, London W1R 9HB. Telephone: 01-629 1206. Telex: 8812664 INBAR G. Fax: 01-409 0456.

Biographies

Ralph Aldwinckle

Chairman of the Law Society of England and Wales' Standing Committee on Company Law, formerly Partner, Linklaters and Paines.

Donald L. Calvin

Chairman of International Business Enterprises Inc., New York, adviser to the Chairman of the Chicago Board Options Exchange and the Geneva Stock Exchange.

Peter Dey

Partner, Osler Hoskin & Harcourt, Toronto and formerly the Chairman of the Ontario Securities Commission.

Jeffrey Knight

Chief Executive of the International Stock Exchange, London. Formerly adviser to the Council for the Securities Industry and special adviser to the Department of Trade and Industry on EEC matters.

Simon macLachlan

From 1964 Partner, Clifford-Turner, and now with the merged firm of Clifford Chance. Vice-chairman of Committee Q of the International Bar Association and a non-executive Director of Continental Can (UK).

Leigh Masel

Consultant to Phillips Fox, solicitors, Melbourne, and McIntosh Hamson Hoare Govett Ltd., stockbrokers, Melbourne. Leigh Masel is also on the Board of Directors of Dun and Bradstreet (Australia) Pty. Ltd., Thomas Cook (Australia) Ltd., National Securities Exchanges Guarantee Corporation Ltd., and Aerospace Technologies of Australia Pty. Ltd. Former Chairman of the Companies and Securities Commission of Australia.

Joni Lysett Nelson

Senior Partner, Rogers & Wells, New York and on the Council of Legal Advisers to the Republican National Committee and the Advisory Board World Trade Institute. Formerly Managing Partner, Rogers & Wells, London.

André Newburg

Partner, Cleary Gottlieb Steen & Hamilton, New York, and Vice-chairman of Committee Q of the Section on Business Law of the International Bar Association.

Noboru Nakagawa

Nakagawa Godo Law Office, Tokyo and a member of the Second Tokyo Bar Association and the International Bar Association.

Gordon Pepper

Director and Senior Adviser of Midland Montagu, London. Formerly Chairman of Greenwell Montagu & Co., and prior to that joint Senior Partner, Greenwell & Co.

Richard Ramsay

Formerly Director of Hill Samuel & Co. Limited in the Bank's Corporate Finance Department.

James A. Riley

Partner, Stikeman Elliott, Toronto, and a frequent speaker at conferences and forums in Canada and the United States.

John W. Robertson

Deputy Chairman of Barclays de Zoete Wedd Securities Ltd., London, and on the Board of the Securities Association. Formerly Deputy Chairman of the Stock Exchange.

J. Michael Robinson, QC

Partner, Fasken Martineau Walker, Toronto, and Chairman of Committee Q. Michael Robinson heads the Fasken & Calvin International Group and was formerly adviser to the Canadian Federal Government with respect to its free trade negotiations with the United States on regulation in Canada of foreign-controlled financial institutions.

Michael Bernard Sayers

Partner, Norton Rose Botterell & Roche and former Editor of the Allied Hambro Investment Guide (now the Allied Dunbar Investment Guide).

A. A. Sommer, Jr.

Partner, Morgan Lewis and Bockius, Washington DC, Chairman of the Public Oversight Board, American Institute of Certified Public Accountants, Chairman of the National Association of Corporate Directors, and Director of Gould Inc., Consolidated Natural Gas Co. and Figgie International Holdings Inc. Formerly a Commissioner of the Securities and Exchange Commission.

Dr. Hans Rudolf Steiner

Partner, Walder Wyss & Partners and Co-Chairman of Committee Q on Issues and Trading in Securities Sub-committee on Current Developments. Former Chairman of the Zurich Bar Association.

Martin J. Vile

Director of the Intermediaries Division of the Securities and Investments Board and responsible for the regulation of collective investment intermediaries and for policy relating to FIMBRA.

Stanislas Yassukovich

Executive Chairman of Merrill Lynch Europe Ltd., London, and Deputy Chairman of the London Stock Exchange. Formerly Group Deputy Chairman of European Banking Group, and Chairman of the Association of International Bond Dealers.

INTRODUCTION

John Salter

(Chairman of the Section on Business Law - International Bar Association)

This Seminar follows the Anugraha Seminar of December last year with the NY Stock Exchange and the International Accounting Standards Committee. It is the 12th seminar during my year of office and is the last one in a whole series of technical seminars which have proved so far to be of a very high standard and enormously successful. The programme reflects the SBL policy of working through a series of informal links, with specialist institutions where those institutions are most likely to help in the work of a committee. In this case of a Committee Q Seminar we welcome the International Stock Exchange, represented by Jeffrey Knight, the New York Stock Exchange represented by Al Sommer, the SIB in London represented by Martin Vile, the Ontario Securities Commission represented by Peter Dey, the Companies Commission of Australia represented by Leigh Masel and the Chicago Board of Options Exchange represented by Donald Calvin. These are just some examples of these informal links and show the mutual benefit of such links both for Committee Q and the various organisations.

Michael Robinson

Many aspects of the Big Bang will be discussed in this seminar. The effects on markets and market efficiency, the effects on market players, new and old self-regulation revisited, new regulations, old regulations revised and the experience of other jurisdictions and other regulators who have undergone, or who are about to undergo a similar process - these things have been done in the United States and Australia and are just in the process of being done in Canada now. Another thing that will be discussed will be that dreaded spectre of whether we will have predatory and unwelcome competition making for instability in the markets and/or the health of the players.

THE CURRENT STATE OF HEALTH OF THE MARKET

Jeffrey Knight

My brief is to talk about the evolution of the market since Big Bang. I will take the events of October, 1986 as read since my learned friend Gordon Pepper will be giving you a profound and perceptive analysis of why Big Bang came to pass in the first place. The only historical aspect on which I want to touch is to remind you of the colossal scale of the change which we undertook to complete by Big Bang day, and the massive extent of the change which took place on that auspicious day. When I look back on what we set ourselves to do I have the same feelings which I have as a parent, contemplating from middle age the antics of my children and forgetting entirely how equally foolhardy were my own antics when I was 19 or so. In other words, if we had had time to contemplate the risks we were running when we decided upon the extent of the changes in Big Bang, we should probably never have dared to start upon that course.

But here we are. We have not only survived but we have by and large prospered, although not every single firm in the market would probably subscribe to that last sentiment.

Perhaps the first thing I should point out is that the UK Stock Exchange is here at all. I mean by that to refer to a moment in the early part of this year when we read in the Financial Times one morning that the New York Stock Exchange had decided that the London Stock Exchange was not to be regarded as an exchange for the purposes of Rule 390 of the New York Stock Exchange rule book. They had read in their newspapers that we had decided that by the end of 1987 trading in equities and gilts would no longer take place on the trading floor. My very good friends in New York then suffered acute discomfiture from the world's press for a week or so while they were ever so mildly ridiculed. In the end, with a masterly sense of realism, Mr. Phelan, the Chairman of the New York Stock Exchange, announced that if the Mother of Parliaments was satisfied that the organisation for which I work and which pays my modest stipend was still to be regarded as a Stock Exchange, then the New York Stock Exchange would be prepared to acknowledge that we should be treated as a Stock Exchange for the purposes of their rules.

It has to be said that the speed of the migration away from the trading floor in London took even the most optimistic amongst us by surprise. I define an optimist in this context as someone who understood and accepted that the dealing system which we had devised to succeed the hallowed and cherished jobbing system was in fact intended to operate on the screen. We expected the sheer conservatism of the financial community to lead to a substantial number of members of the Stock Exchange clinging to the old ways and continuing to use the floor, and for that reason alone we had carried out a large and exceedingly expensive project to bring onto the trading floor the same electronic devices which were being installed in the offices of member firms. As it turned out, the members deserted the floor with quite astonishing alacrity, and trading had effectively finished on the trading floor by the end of 1986. Nowadays only the Traded Options market functions there, together with a few retail brokers in gilts who find it convenient to stay in the old market.

So the physical manifestation of the stock market disappeared almost overnight. The Stock Exchange remains on the tourist route and visitors continue to flock into our gallery, where their attention has to be diverted away from the empty floor to where they are invited to look at videos and other modern aids to comprehension.

The migration from the floor can equally be regarded as clear evidence of the success of the massive technological changes we made to enable our very large market to function on the screen. You will no doubt remember the embarrassing technical fault which affected our TOPIC service on the very morning of Big Bang itself, and to which the world's press drew gleeful attention. We did have a technical problem, which was essentially one of capacity, and which caused us grave embarrassment for two or three days, but which was then cured and has only cropped up two or three times since. The SEAQ system, which is at the heart of the dealing system, which takes in quotations from market-makers and displays the market some thousands of stocks on the screen, has operated since November last at well over 99% reliability. In systems terms, I am informed by my technically educated colleagues that this is a success rate almost impossible to surpass.

You may also remember that the SEAQ system was modelled on the NASDAQ systems in the United States, with which many of you are very familiar. Well, we did take NASDAQ as our model, distinguishing between a system relying upon competing market-makers and one where the auction method is the basis of price formation, and we were able to do so because we had already in existence a private network of our own, called TOPIC, which carried market prices on several thousand securities. TOPIC had at that time, when we started planning for Big Bang, some 2,500 terminals, which I believe is about the total terminal population of the NASDAQ system. We have today rather more than 13,000 terminals receiving the UK equity market on TOPIC. If other quote vendors are counted in, the number is more than 18,000. It is, in other words, a very much larger network to support than is NASDAQ, on which SEAQ was modelled.

You may remember that the changes which became known as Big Bang had three essential elements. They were the abolition of fixed minimum commission rates for Stock Exchange trading, the introduction of the screen-based dealing system I have just been describing, and the broadening of the Stock Exchange membership. In the event it is the last of these three which will prove to be the most profound in its repercussions.

There is now virtually no barrier to entry to the London Stock Exchange. Access to the market can be obtained either directly, by suitably qualified and capitalised entities, or by the acquisition of an existing member firm. Almost all of the larger member firms have been bought either in their entirety or as to a substantial majority, and a good many small firms have also passed into the control of non-member institutions. Entry costs have been deliberately set at a moderate level, and there are no seats to be acquired. Virtually no restriction has been placed upon foreign ownership of member firms, and to illustrate that, at the most recent count there were 345 corporate member firms of which 74 were foreign owned. There are still some 5,300 individual members but the membership have voted to give up their individual voting rights, and voting is now controlled by corporate members. (This change was effected only with a considerable amount of pain and distress by the individual members). Another notable feature of the new membership is that it is now almost entirely corporate, where previously by far the greatest number of member firms were partnerships.

We decided in the course of planning for Big Bang that the Stock Exchange should be organised along the lines of the four quite separate markets which it provides. They are the market in government bonds or gilt-edged; the market in UK or domestic equities; the market in Traded Options; and the market in foreign equities, about which I will say a bit more in a moment. I will describe very briefly each market in turn.

The Stock Exchange has always had a very broad market in our own domestic equities. There are now some 1,800 equity securities of UK companies officially listed on the Exchange and another 350 traded on the Unlisted Securities Market (USM). In January this year, for reasons partly connected with the regulatory changes, we introduced a formal market in the Exchange for what had previously been traded over the counter, and we called it the Third Market. This market is intended for companies without the usual record of trading which is required to support a listing or admission to the USM, and 23 companies have been admitted to the Third Market.

Previously, the most dramatic market development since Big Bang has been the growth in the size of the market in UK stocks. The daily turnover figures before Big Bang were of the order of 27,500 transactions with an average value of £650m. The average daily turnover in the first three months after Big Bang was £840m, or 30% above the daily average turnover over the first nine months of 1986. Turnover has subsequently risen to sustained levels of 60,000 transactions and £1.5b per day. The highest recorded day was £2.05b. We have become quite accustomed to trading and settling over 600 million shares per day.

Mention of settlement brings with it a more sombre note. With the explosion in trading volumes and values there has developed a concomitant problem in the back offices of member firms and institutions which has left substantial amounts of business delayed in settlement for what are now quite unacceptable periods of time. It is a relief, but no particular pleasure, to record that the central settlement systems of the Stock Exchange, which were upgraded in order to cope with much higher volumes than we had last year, have stood up extraordinarily well. The fact is, however, that the City at large has been found to be short of the back office capacity to settle the amounts of business which have been generated at the dealing desk. Recognising the seriousness of the settlement backlog, and knowing something of the trauma caused by these things in Wall Street in the late 1960's, we have set about extinguishing the backlog, but it is a long and difficult task. The problems will not go away quickly.

A very notable feature of the equity market since Big Bang has been the volume of new issues and, of course, the enormous impact of the UK Government privatisation issues. The first of these to have a major impact on the British public was British Telecom nearly three years ago, but in the period covered by this paper we have seen the Trustee

Savings Bank sale, British Gas, British Airways, Rolls Royce and British Airports Authority. The number of individual shareholders in this country which five years ago was estimated at two and a half million is now thought to be closer to eight and a half million. In the Autumn we will see the sale of the last tranche of the British Government's holding in British Petroleum, expected to realise £7.5b, the biggest equity offering ever made anywhere in the world, and the extent of the publicity being given to that event seems likely to ensure a further broadening of the shareholder base in this country.

I must say a little about the Traded Options market. We started a market in Traded Options in April, 1978 at about the time the European Options Exchange opened in Amsterdam. Our market remained very small until, with the advent of the Big Bang changes, it became a byword that with substantially greater risk positions being taken by intermediaries in the equity market, facilities for hedging would be required. In consequence, the volume of trade in Traded Options has increased dramatically since 1985. In that year 900,000 contracts were traded. In 1986 5.3 million contracts were traded and in the first eight months of 1987 over 8 million contracts have been traded. The market, with new classes and instruments being constantly added, is growing at a rate of about 9% per month.

I am aware that the language I have been using is full of superlatives and might be thought prone to exaggeration. I do not want to apologise or withdraw anything I have said, and when I turn to the Foreign Equity Market I have once again to reach for my Thesaurus and look for some more expansive words. But a short further digression is needed.

When, in the second half of 1985, it was borne in on the international financial community in London that they were going to be profoundly affected by the then forthcoming legislation, they very rapidly decided that something had to be done. It is now a matter of history that what they did was to form an organisation called ISRO which united the

London subsidiaries and branches of many of the most powerful securities houses in the world. Almost equally rapidly it occurred to them, and at the same time to us at the Stock Exchange, that to set up two different SROs to supervise what is essentially the same business would be wasteful, and during 1986 we negotiated a merger of the firms which formed ISRO with the old UK Stock Exchange. The result is proudly known as the International Stock Exchange of the United Kingdom and the Republic of Ireland. The name is no idle boast. We do quite plainly intend to create what will be the first real international stock exchange, capable of embracing a wide and powerful international membership, and of trading the shares of all the great international stocks in the world.

The marriage of the Stock Exchange and ISRO has in fact produced twin offspring in the shape of the International Stock Exchange and the Securities Association. The latter has applied for recognition as an SRO in the terms of the Act.

The Stock Exchange's Foreign Equity Market is the most vital manifestation of that merger. It is well-understood that there has for some time been an active market made over the counter and over the telephone in non-UK shares in London. The Financial Services Act makes it desirable to bring that trading within a regulated exchange framework and the Foreign Equity Market is being created to provide that part of our RIE which will trade non-UK shares on a regulated and visible basis.

SEAQ International, which is the vehicle for the marketing in Foreign Equities, was in fact introduced in mid 1985, almost 18 months before Big Bang. It now shows prices in some 790 foreign equities, in 190 of which firm two-way prices are quoted. Rules are being devised and introduced for trading in this market and reporting of trades has started in the Dutch, French, Japanese, German, South African, Scandinavian and Canadian sectors. At the moment we publish the volumes in all these except for the French and German ones, where only the weekly totals are published, but we intend that trade reporting and publication of trade volumes should be introduced in all the sectors before the end of the year.

I will leave the gilt-edged market to Mr. Pepper whose professional field it very much is.

The essence of the new dual capacity market-making system for equities is that large, well-capitalised firms are engaged in both agency broking and in making markets. As market-makers, registered in many cases in a wide-range of stocks, they are given privileges, including tax advantages, in return for assuring obligations to deal with all other member firms at the quoted price for the size of transactions indicated. The fact that there are now 33 equity market-makers compared to the 13 firms of jobbers, only 5 of which were of any significant size, indicates that the market has become much more competitive since Big Bang.

The securities for which prices are quoted on SEAQ are divided into four groups - alpha securities which are identified as being the securities which have 10 or more market-makers and whose turnover represents at least £100m per quarter; beta securities which have at least six market-makers, gamma securities which have two market-makers and other listed securities known as delta securities. The turnover within each of these sectors was such that alpha securities (of which there are at present 102) represented 56.1% of turnover post Big Bang, whilst the levels for betas, gammas and deltas stood at 34.3%, 7.2% and 2.4% respectively. When the market touches - that is, the difference between the best bid and the best offer price prevailing in a security - were considered, the alpha securities were found to have relatively narrow touches whilst the betas and gammas with slightly less liquid markets had somewhat wider spreads.

The touch prices in a sample of alpha stocks were found to have been reduced to 0.73% post Big Bang, whilst the figures for beta stocks have reduced for large lot quotations to 1.66%. The touch prices for gamma securities have been stable between 2.4% and 2.7% in small size transactions and falling gradually for larger transactions.

Since Big Bang, a team of people have been monitoring the quality of the market. Their analysis has shown that for each SEAQ category there has been a reduction in the size premium post Big Bang. That is to say that much larger transaction sizes can be carried out at little or no change in market touch, thus emphasising the enhanced depth of the market.

Market Structure

One of the principal components of the reform of the market was the move to fully negotiable commission rates. The Stock Exchange has, of course, been monitoring the effect of this change on the market and in December, 1986 an extensive survey was conducted. The results of this survey shows that in the majority of cases, commission charges for the private client have remained similar to pre-Big Bang levels, although some 20% of firms offered rates lower than the minimum scale in all sizes of transactions. Having said that, it should be stressed that not all firms will be offering the same service and differences will be reflected in the commission charge. Comparing the average commission scale with the minimum scale (for bargains up to £20,000), the results of the survey indicate that commission rates have been reduced by approximately 3%. It should, however, be noted that some transactions such as the closing of a position dealt within a stock exchange account period, were transacted free of commission.

About 80% of the turnover value in customer business in equities is reckoned to be institutional business. Although exact figures on the commission charges being paid for this type of business are not available I would estimate that around 50% of it is being dealt directly with a market-maker at a net price (that is, no commission is being charged).

For the remainder of institutional business which is subject to commissions, the rate charged is negotiable and ranges from 0.5% to 0.2% with a few very large deals being done at 0.125%.

Perhaps the most dramatic way of illustrating the extent and nature of what has happened to the old London Stock Exchange is to refer to the manner in which it is now governed. If the old Stock Exchange was a club - in the best sense - then the Council of the Stock Exchange was a club within a club. The terms of the merger with ISRO in November last year provided that there should be two governing bodies, one to prepare the application to become an SRO: this as you may know is called the Securities Association; the other, the Council of the Stock Exchange, is making an application to become an RIE. Each of the two bodies was and is composed half and half of the representatives of ISRO and the old Stock Exchange, with the addition, in each case, of a number of lay representatives. The Stock Exchange Council now has four Americans, two Japanese, two Canadians and representatives of French, German, Australian and Swiss securities houses. That is the best testimony I can adduce to the true international nature of the old London Stock Exchange.

SOME ECONOMIC REASONS FOR BIG BANG AND THE NEW GILT-EDGED MARKET

Gordon Pepper

My remarks will be in two parts - first, the new gilt-edged market and, second, some general comments about Big Bang.

Jeffrey Knight has explained how our new equity market was modelled on NASDAQ. Our new gilt-edged market has, in contrast, been modelled on the US Government bond market. US citizens amongst you will appreciate that the structures of the equity and bond markets are very different. Prices of bonds are not quoted over a common viewdata network available to everyone. The bond markets are based on competing view data networks provided by the specialist inter-dealer brokers. These networks provide the ultimate of real time reporting of what is happening in the heart of the market, and the clever feature is that they do so in a way which does not disclose dealers' underlying positions. The screens are not, however, available to anyone who is not registered with the Bank of England as a gilt-edged market-maker, i.e. as a primary dealer. In this respect, the gilt-edged market is inferior to our equity market.

The new market has been a great success for users of the market. Dealing spreads have dropped substantially and commission has virtually disappeared on institutional business. The cost of transacting business is best measured by the difference between the net price received by a seller and that paid by the buyer. Before Big Bang, it averaged just over 1/4% for transactions larger than £250,000 in long dated bonds. If a bond is a "runner" i.e. one which is frequently traded, the difference is now 1/16% (i.e. it is a quarter of what it used to be). Turnover has increased very substantially but a lot of itis between the gilt-edged market-makers. If this is excluded, turnover has increased by more than two-thirds compared with a year ago, and by about 100% compared with two years ago. So, the new market is both more liquid and cheaper than the old, which is good for its users. The doubt is about the profitability of market-makers. Twenty six of them is too many. According to rumour, market-makers as a whole have lost about £100m since the Big Bang. Lloyds Bank has already withdrawn. Others will follow. That is all I am going to say about the gilt-edged market; elaboration can be left until the discussion.

I want to make four general points about the Big Bang. The first is to emphasise the degree of change. The Big Bang was much more than just the abolition of minimum commissions on the Stock Exchange, London's version of the change that occurred in New York on May Day 1975. It was also more than an alteration in the structure of the Stock Exchange - a breakdown of the old separation of market-makers (whom we call jobbers) from agents (our brokers). To appreciate the extent of the change, the old structure of the City of London should be contrasted with that of other leading financial centres.

In the United States, commercial banks are separate from investment banks. In Japan too there is a similar separation between a banking licence and a securities licence. On the continent of Europe, in contrast, there is no such separation; there are universal banks. In Britain the old structure of the City of London was different again. It was based on specialist financial institutions, stockbrokers, stockjobbers (the market-makers) discount houses (specialists in the money and bill markets), merchant banks and our very large clearing banks (retail banks) with their country-wide branch networks.

The Big Bang was about changing the whole structure of the City of London from specialisation to either US type investment banking or continental universal banking. It was a total upheaval.

Interestingly, having resisted changes we have leap-frogged over New York and are now leading it in two important respects. First, our stock exchange has been thrown open virtually to all-comers, and the cost of entry has been kept low, as Jeffrey Knight has explained. Second, US commercial banks in London can experiment with investment banking; they can practice what they hope soon to be able to do at home.

My second point is that the driving force behind the change was technology. The securities industry is one of the main beneficiaries of the communications and information revolution. The Office of Fair Trading's referral of the Stock Exchange to the Restrictive Practice Court was, in my opinion, a minor factor. The abolition of exchange controls was much more important. This allowed the international securities houses in London which had adopted the modern technology to steal business from our domestic firms. We were faced with a stark choice of either preserving the old way of life and rapidly losing market share or of changing to the new technology. We chose the latter.

My third point is the cost of the technology. If an investment bank/securities house is ambitious, and plans to have a presence in New York and Tokyo as well as in London, the total systems budget, including development expenditure, should nowadays probably be of the order of £100m p.a. Many small and medium-sized firms will not be able to stay in the race. We have suddenly changed from being a boutique industry to big business.

My fourth point is that this change to big business throws up enormous problems for management. We are not only merging small firms with large, but firms with totally different cultures, and the cultures are often incompatible.

There used to be a law in the United Kingdom restricting partnerships to 20. About five years after it was rescinded, I think in the early 1970s, I remember well a meeting at which the senior partners of the large firms of solicitors, accountants and stockbrokers compared notes about how to run large partnerships - no matter the profession, the problems had a lot in common. Since then, we have gone our different ways. Many of the accountants have expanded into mammoth international partnerships. The lawyers have tended to keep more to their national boundaries. The stockbrokers have gone corporate and then become part of much larger businesses.

I would suggest to you that the evolution of management techniques is the most interesting by-product of the Big Bang happening in London at the moment. How do we combine the formal procedures and disciplines which are essential in large organisations with the need to create an environment in which professional people can thrive? Time will tell which management style proves to be the most effective. London is a vast experiment. Other professions would be wise to observe what is happening and decide whether the successful recipe, which will be thrown up by the market place in due course, is relevant for them.

Simon macLachlan

I have one question Jeffrey which I might raise with you. When the Chancellor recently increased interest rates there were a lot of rumours about the fact that market-makers at the end of telephone lines were not answering the telephone and one wonders whether Mr. Phelan's view that you had to be face to face to have a proper market had some truth in it. Was that just a quirk of one day or is it a concern raised by a different sort of market?

Answer

I think what you are saying is that it was alleged that market-makers were not answering their telephones and were not then able to take on the selling orders that the brokers had when the news of the rising interest rates occurred. Well, the answer to that is rather a complicated one. There was a period of time, it lasted a couple of hours in the middle of the day, when the market changed very, very rapidly and we had to cope with that in systems terms.

Price changes were coming in all the time and the people in the offices who make the prices and deal are the same ones who have to change prices and so they were busier adjusting their own prices on which they are obliged to deal. The prices which they post on the screens which for the most part in the big stocks are very, very large indeed are the prices with which they are obliged to deal and because they were assessing the impact of the news which was coming over the wires about interest rates they were not easily about to answer the phone and deal. We invented the expression for those sort of circumstances as a 'fast market' and we will have to find ways in which we can accommodate the need for the market to adjust itself very rapidly. In fact, to compare the position with the trading floor and to suggest that the market dealing over the telephone is less effective in that regard is probably illusory because even when the chaps were meeting eyeball-to-eyeball on the trading floor if it underwent a sudden flux - such as happened when the interest rate changes were announced - the jobbers who were equally obliged to deal with allcomers had ways of protecting themselves and if they wanted to widen their spreads or just go and have a cup of coffee while they thought about it that was always possible. So, it is real life, chaps do have to think about things and we have to accommodate them within the rules.

THE LEGAL FRAMEWORK FOR THE REGULATION OF INVESTMENT BUSINESS UNDER THE FINANCIAL SERVICES ACT 1986

Timothy J. Herrington

1. Introduction

The Financial Services Act 1986 ("the Act") received the Royal Assent on 7th November, 1986. Most of it remains to be implemented and it is looking increasingly as if it will not be fully in force until the spring of next year.

The Act has been widely hailed as the most wide-ranging and ambitious piece of securities legislation ever introduced in the United Kingdom. This is certainly true, because the whole range of financial activities in the City of London is affected by it. However, it could fairly be said that its ambition has, to at least some extent, outstripped its abilities. Much of the detail of the new regime has yet to be settled and promulgated by means of various rule books, and some of the detail which is contained in the Act is not so much complex as almost unintelligible and forbidding even for professional advisers. Indeed, when visiting a client for the first time to outline the implications of the Act, I sometimes feel like the poor messenger who in classical times brought news of the results of the latest battle to his sovereign; if the news was bad the messenger would be executed!

2. What the Act Regulates

In fact, the focal provision of the Act is almost the shortest. Section 3 states that no person shall carry on investment business in the United Kingdom unless he is an authorised person or an exempted person under the Act. Section 4 then explains that carrying on an investment business without authorisation or exemption will render the offender liable to imprisonment of up to two years, or to a potentially unlimited fine, or both. Just as significantly, by virtue of section 5 an offender will find that he is unable to enforce any agreement made by him in contravention of the prohibition without an order of the court, while his counterparty will be able to recover any money paid or property transferred to him, unless he chooses to hold the unauthorised person to the agreement.

Participants in the UK securities markets therefore need to ask themselves if they are carrying on (or purporting to carry on) investment business in the United Kingdom. If the answer to the first question is "yes" or, quite possibly, "perhaps" it will be necessary to investigate how to become authorised, a topic which Michael Sayers will deal with shortly.

To answer the first question it is necessary to refer to the detailed provisions of Schedule 1 to the Act and ask the following questions:

- Does the transaction in question concern investments?
- Is there an investment activity?
- Does it amount to a business?
- Is it carried on from a permanent place of business in the United Kingdom or engaged in in the United Kingdom?

If the answer to all of these questions is "yes" authorisation or an exemption will be required subject to numerous complicated exclusions designed to ensure, for instance, that those whose main business is not investment business but who also deal in investments (such as the treasury department of an industrial company and those who deal as principal on their own account) do not require authorisation.

Broadly speaking the term "investment" is very widely defined and includes:

- all types of securities and interests in securities, such as shares, bonds, notes, debentures, certificates of deposit, government and public securities, depositary receipts, warrants, options and units in collective investment schemes;

- currency and other financial options, options on gold and silver and options on commodity futures;

  delivery based futures (but not where the contract is made for purely commercial purposes otherwise than on a recognised investment exchange);

- contracts for differences, including index based futures contracts, interest rate and currency swap agreements; and

- most long-term insurance contracts.

Wide-ranging as the definitions in Schedule 1 may be, there are some rather surprising omissions. Thus, many items which are commonly spoken of and regarded as investments do not fall with the statutory definition. Physical items, such as postage stamps, rare coins, works of art and land and other real property, are not included, so that their sale and promotion would only be covered insofar as interests in them were promoted through a collective investment scheme such as a property or commodity unit trust or they were sold in such a way as to bring them into the category of "futures". There does not seem to be any very obvious reason for these omissions, and one would have thought that there was just as much scope for malpractice (and, therefore, just as much need of regulation) in those fields as there were in relation to the investments which are specified in the Schedule. In order to deal with anomalies (of which this may be one) and to provide a flexible statutory response to the changing face of the markets, the Secretary of State may amend the statutory definition of "investment" so as to extend or restrict it.

One can see in clear relief the effect of not having the equivalent of a Glass-Steagall Act in the United Kingdom; many of the instruments dealt in by commercial banks will be classed as investments; indeed the definition of debenture is so wide (it is stated in terms of including virtually any instrument creating or acknowledging indebtedness) that it is very difficult to convince oneself in all logic that a simple loan agreement is not capable of being classified as a debenture and thus an investment, and that as a result all mainstream banking business is also investment business. Lawyers are tending to take a common sense approach, however, and do not treat this as being the case, although we became more concerned where the loan is represented by transferable pieces of paper.

Having defined "investment" it is necessary to refer to the next two or three parts of Schedule 1 to see whether the activities in question constitute "investment business". "Business" is supposed to be construed fairly robustly, but that does not mean that only persons whose main or only business involves investments are affected. All that is required for there to be a business is a recurring source of profit, although one judge has said in a case that "almost anything which is an occupation or duty which requires attention is a business" - a much wider construction.

The "investment activities" which are relevant are:

- dealings in investments;
- arranging deals in investments;
- managing investments;

- advising persons in their capacity as investors or potential investors on the merits of particular investments; and
- operating a collective investment scheme such as a unit trust.

3. The Impact of the Act on Overseas Persons

The foregoing is an attempt to summarise the effect of over 10 pages of closely typed statutory provisions and without any difficulty we could spend the rest of the day analysing the scope of such phrases as "arranging deals", "advising persons on the merits of particular investments" and "contracts for differences" - a true lawyer's delight. Rather than attempt to do that briefly, it may be of interest to the reader to dwell on how the Act affects those from overseas who carry on investment activities with or through persons in the United Kingdom; as we have seen the Act bites on persons doing so even without a permanent place of business in the United Kingdom and thus the provisions are given something of an extraterritorial flavour.

To recap, the Act makes it clear that a person carries on investment business in the United Kingdom if either:

(a) he carries on that business from a permanent place of business maintained by him in the United Kingdom; or

(b) he engages in the United Kingdom in one or more of the activities which I have described and his doing so constitutes the carrying on by him of a business in the United Kingdom.

By way of illustration, if an American broker takes offices in London and starts to deal in securities whether on a branch office basis or having formed a separate subsidiary, he is carrying on investment business in the

United Kingdom. If he has no office here but solicits UK customers by letter or telephone from the States and enters into transactions with them, he satisfies the definition just as much as if he had been physically resident here. On the other hand, activities of a peripheral or preliminary nature such as customer liaison or research and monitoring facilities conducted in the United Kingdom probably do not require authorisation, either because there is no "business" as such or because none of the activities exactly fit into the heads contained in Part II of Schedule 1, for example the supply of information or ratings about securities which does not amount to investment advice.

Mention was made briefly above of a number of exclusions, such as own account dealing, which are available equally to UK and overseas businesses. However, there are additional exclusions which are available only to overseas businesses and which, when analysed, seem to confer a very wide power to operate in the United Kingdom which is not available to UK domestic businesses. It should be noted that these exclusions follow representations from a number of quarters during the parliamentary passage of the Financial Services Bill. The results, however, are considerably in excess of anything one could reasonably have hoped for on behalf of a client seeking to do business on equal terms with his UK counterpart. The exclusions can be summarised as follows:

(1) Transactions with or through Authorised or Exempted Persons

The exclusions are contained in paragraphs 26 and 27 of Schedule 1. I will deal with them in turn, I hope without getting too technical in an area of unbelievable complexity. The overriding point to make is that they cover businesses which have no permanent place of establishment in the United Kingdom from which investment business is conducted, and therefore will never be available if a business has offices here or uses the premises of another investment house on a continuous basis.

Paragraph 26 states that the activity of dealing in investments is not to be treated as an investment business in relation to any transaction by an overseas person with or through either an authorised person or an exempted person. So this means that if there is an authorised person (whom I will call "Geoffrey") in the United Kingdom prepared to act as intermediary, the overseas person (whom I will call "Ivan") can enter into transactions here untrammelled by regulations. The catch, of course, is that Geoffrey is the one who needs to comply with the Act and the relevant rules made under it.

The exclusion covers "arranging deals" as well as dealing. For example, if Ivan decides he wants to offer corporate finance activities, bringing together buyer and seller or lender and borrower without himself necessarily being party as a principal to any transaction, he can do so provided Geoffrey is involved. He may advertise his services or call upon intended customers so long as the arrangements are made through Geoffrey.

(2) Unsolicited Transactions

A separate set of exclusions exist in paragraph 27. These embrace all the activities which are capable of constituting investment business, not just dealing or arranging. The requirements of authorisation do not apply if the transaction, offer, agreement, or advice of Ivan is the result of:

<u>First</u> - an approach made <u>to</u> Ivan <u>by</u> or on behalf of a UK customer <u>which either</u> has not been in any way solicited by Ivan or has been solicited by him in a way which does not contravene sections 56 or 57 of the Act; <u>or</u>

Second - an approach made by Ivan which manages not to contravene either of those sections.

Sections 56 and 57 are all about cold-calling and advertising, and these activities are prohibited unless conducted in a particular way or with particular people. Before I explain how they work, let me summarise the effect of paragraph 27. It appears to be that if Ivan receives a call from a UK person and he has done nothing to solicit it, then he is perfectly free to transact business with that person without the intervention of a UK authorised intermediary such as Geoffrey. And again, if Ivan has done the soliciting or advertising but in a way that does not infringe sections 56 or 57, then by the same token he can enter into transactions quite freely with UK customers.

In case you think this is all perfectly reasonable, let me emphasise that except in the anomalous situation mentioned below, a UK investment business could not enter into commitments on these terms. It is not open for Geoffrey to set up as an investment broker and simply use the good offices of an authorised intermediary to market a range of services or sign contract notes on his behalf. In these circumstances generally he would need to be separately authorised as a UK investment business. Similarly, there is no rule which says that a UK investment business that does not solicit clients, or solicits them in such a way that statutory rules as to advertising and cold-calling are not broken, can carry on without authorisation. If that were so, it would enable UK businesses to conduct operations quite happily with other professional or business investors without going near the doors of the Securities Investment Board or a Self-regulating Organisation. That is not how the legislation works. While it is true that there are certain relaxations in the Conduct of Business Rules for authorised persons dealing with professionals, no transactions can take place until an authorisation is in place. The overseas person thus has a distinct advantage to participate in London investment markets provided he does not establish a permanent place of business here. That in itself will be a modest handicap, but it could certainly keep the Atlantic airlines in profit as agents and customers wing their way backwards and forwards between New York and London.

The anomaly mentioned above is that, because of the curious way paragraph 27 is worded, any transaction entered into by an overseas person with a person in the United Kingdom which has not been solicited unlawfully by the overseas person is excluded from the control of the Act. Thus, it would be possible for a person to set up business in the United Kingdom and deal only with overseas persons and not need authorisation, notwithstanding that he had a place of business in the United Kingdom - the exclusion only ceases to be available if the overseas person has a place of business in the United Kingdom. Thus, it would be possible for an overseas business to set up a UK dealing subsidiary and run it quite lawfully without authorisation provided it dealt only with overseas persons and did not need to solicit business in a way which contravened section 56 or section 57.

4. Cold-calling

I must now deal, by way of a huge parenthesis, with sections 56 and 57 of the Act. These are the teeth of the new legislation for both UK and overseas persons and a firm who tries to enter into an investment agreement with the likes of you and me without complying with them is not going to get very far, because none of his contracts will be enforceable without an order of the court.

Cold-calling refers to personal visits or oral communications made without express invitation. Section 56 imposes a prohibition on persons attempting to accomplish investment business during or in consequence of an unsolicited call made on a person in the United Kingdom or from the United Kingdom on a person elsewhere. This means that I can no longer be sold a dubious savings plan by an itinerant salesman while I am sitting by the River Thames eating my sandwiches.

The Act only allows three exceptions from the general ban:

Firstly - calls on professional or business investors;

Secondly - calls where the contract can be cancelled under the Cancellation Rules made under section 59 of the Act. The SIB currently intends that these rules should cover life assurance products and possibly unit trusts;

Thirdly - calls made on a person with whom the caller has a written agreement which contemplates unsolicited calls. In practice, permission will be contained in client agreements. This exemption will not cover existing clients or customers with whom there is no such written agreement, however many transactions they may have done with or through the firm before.

The new law will impose tougher restrictions on cold-calling than is now the case. Dealers in securities, commodities and financial futures will not be able to cold-call non-professional customers unless the customer has agreed, in writing, to be called on in this way. Where cold-calling is permitted, it must be undertaken in accordance with strict ethical standards.

In order not to place unreasonable or unnecessary restraints on firms wishing to advertise their services, the prohibition on cold-calling relates only to uninvited personal calls and oral communications. It does not relate to sending letters or mail shots to potential clients. These will be permitted as a traditional means of attracting business, unless the circularisation amounts to sending investment advertisements which are separately regulated.

5. Restrictions on Advertising

Section 57 provides that subject to a series of exemptions, no person, other than an authorised person, shall issue or cause to be issued an investment advertisement in the United Kingdom unless its contents have been approved by an authorised person. Advertisements issued outside the United Kingdom are treated as issued in the United Kingdom if they are directed at persons here otherwise than in an overseas newspaper. Advertising is defined to include "every form of advertising whether in a publication, by the display of notices, signs, labels or show cards, by means of circulars, catalogues, price lists or other documents, by an exhibition of pictures, or photographic or cinematographic films, by way of sound broadcasting or television, or in any other manner."

The prohibitions of section 57 will be narrowed by statutory order to be issued by the Secretary of State under section 58(3). The exemptions will be available to:

(i) advertisements of a private character; or

(ii) advertisements dealing only incidentally with investments; or

(iii) advertisements issued to persons appearing to be sufficiently expert to understand the risks involved; or

(iv) such other classes of advertisements as the Secretary of State thinks fit.

Company prospectuses are, of course, investment advertisements. If the prospectus relates to listed securities, then Part IV of the Act applies rather than section 57 and, Ralph Aldwinckle will no doubt enlarge on this, the advertisement must be approved by the Stock Exchange or take the form of listing particulars. For unlisted securities, Part V will eventually apply in substitution for the Companies Act 1985 so that documents blessed by an approved exchange and registered as prospectuses may be lawfully issued.

I hope this brief survey has provided a taste of the complex legal framework that will govern the operations of investment businesses in the United Kingdom when the Act is fully implemented, and has helped to explain why many people are of the view that the only people really to benefit from this legislation will be the lawyers.

Michael Sayers

I shall explain the legal framework under the Financial Services Act 1986 for the authorisation of investment businesses and then Martin Vile will explain (from his superior vantage point) how it will really work.

The first point that I should make is that although before the Financial Services Act emerged, people (including practitioners) might have been pardoned if they had thought that self-regulation meant much the same thing as informal regulation, nobody could think that nowadays. The kind of self-regulation which the Act is calling into being is just about as complex and legalistic as anything that could possible be imagined.

Tim Herrington has explained what, for the purposes of the Act, constitutes an investment and investment business respectively, and that the authorisation provisions of the Act apply to any investment business carried on in the United Kingdom. Special provisions, contained in section 31 of the Act, authorise the carrying on of investment business in the United Kingdom by persons who are authorised to carry it on in other member states of the EEC.

Anyone who carries on an investment business in the United Kingdom must either be authorised or be exempted under the Act. Exemption only applies in very limited circumstances, described in sections 35 to 46 inclusive of the Act. However, it is perhaps important to note that so-called recognised investment exchanges and recognised clearing houses, as well as the Society of Lloyds, are exempted persons. I will not say anything more about exempted persons.

If authorisation is needed, it must be obtained. To carry on an investment business without authorisation is a criminal offence. Contracts entered into by an unauthorised person carrying on investment business will normally be unenforceable and there are other legal sanctions that also exist. In addition, section 62 of the Act confers wide-ranging rights of action, i.e. civil proceedings, "at the suit of a person who suffers loss as a result of [a] contravention" either of rules or regulations made by the Secretary of State for Trade and Industry (who has the ultimate responsibility for the administration of the Act) or by members of SROs or persons certified by RPBs under their respective rules.

As to the methods of becoming authorised, they can be summarised as follows:

- In the first place, the Securities and Investments Board (SIB) - which is the body established under the Act to carry out most of the regulatory functions, and of which incidentally, Martin Vile is a senior executive - may itself directly authorise "fit and proper persons" to carry on investment. However, everyone expects that the SIB will exercise this power extremely sparingly and, on the whole, mainly in circumstances where someone is proposing to carry out a type of investment business which does not readily fall within the ambit of one of the recognised self-regulating organisations (SROs). Quite apart from anything else, the SIB does not have, and does not intend to have, the elaborate bureaucratic structure which would be needed if it were to be able to process thousands of direct applications to it for authorisation.

\- When one comes to speak of membership of an SRO one is getting close to concepts which were well-known in the corporatist states of continental Europe, both in the 1930s and perhaps more recently, but which have been relatively rare in the Anglo-Saxon world. There are to be a strictly limited number of SROs, and membership of one of them will mean that the member who is carrying on, or who is proposing to carry on, an investment business will automatically be authorised in relation to the activities which fall within the scope of the particular SRO of which he is a member.

For an SRO to qualify for recognition, it will have to satisfy the SIB that its rules provide investors with protection which is at least equivalent to that which is provided by the SIB's own rules and that the SRO has effective arrangements for monitoring and enforcing compliance with those rules.

In principle, each recognised SRO will normally regulate only certain types of investment business; and its rules will be required to restrict its members to the carrying on of those types of business, but as respects other investment business which the members of a particular SRO may wish to carry on, those members may elect to join another SRO or may seek direct authorisation by the SIB.

One key requirement is that, as a condition of membership of the SRO concerned, members must submit to it business plans showing their current and their intended investment activities and they will be required to adhere to these plans.

Since, as previously mentioned, some investment businesses may find it necessary to belong to more than one SRO, the SIB will recognise one SRO as a "lead regulator" and it will be that SRO which will, for instance, prescribe the capital adequacy requirements for the particular investment business.

Almost all the SROs have truly forbidding acronyms by which in practice they are known. The emerging SROs, at this moment in time, are the Association of Futures Brokers and Dealers (AFBD), the Financial Intermediaries, Managers and Brokers Regulatory Association (FIMBRA), the Investment Management Regulatory Organisation (IMRO), which concentrates on collective management schemes, the Life Assurance and Unit Trust Regulatory Organisation (LAUTRO) and, perhaps the most important of all, the Securities Association (TSA), to which most members of the Stock Exchange will belong. Each SRO has its own rule book, which in every case, and in more than one sense, could be described as a weighty document.

Another form of authorisation is certification by a recognised professional body, or RPB. Various professionals, including particular solicitors and accountants, carry on some investment business as an incidental or an ancillary part of their professional practice. Such professionals are of course already subject to the disciplinary and other requirements of their respective professional bodies and the Act allows those bodies to apply for recognition. If a professional body is recognised, then any person certified by that body will ipso facto be authorised to carry on investment business. Any professional body seeking recognition of this kind (which is granted by the SIB) must have rules which afford to investors protection which is at least equivalent to that afforded by the rules applicable to persons directly authorised by the SIB, and the professional body's rules must also ensure that certification is limited to members who carry on investment business only incidentally to the practice of their profession.

Insurance companies and friendly societies. These are of course regulated under their own statutes, namely the Insurance Companies Act 1982 and the Friendly Societies Act 1974. They have automatic authorisation to carry on investment business.

I should mention one well-known organisation which, as matters currently stand, is not within the regulatory framework prescribed by the Act at all, namely the Panel on Take-overs and Mergers. The Panel has succeeded, for the time being at least, in retaining its cherished status as a non-statutory regulator. However, that status is now subject to two important qualifications:

(a) In the first place, it is now established law, following the Datafin case in 1986, that the Panel's rulings are subject to judicial review by the courts, even though it is also clear from the judgment in that case that the power of judicial review will be exercised sparingly.

(b) Secondly, the SROs, and the SIB, are writing into their rule books provisions to the effect that members are obliged to comply with the City Code on Take-overs and Mergers (the City Code comprises, of course, the regulations which the Panel administers). It could be said that by this indirect means the provisions of the City Code are being given virtually the force of law, in certain circumstances anyway, even though the body which primarily administers the Code, namely the Panel, is not a recognised regulator. This very English arrangement may perhaps not survive for many years.

I have tried to summarise, in the brief time available, the principal elements of a distinctly unusual regulatory structure. That structure is still emerging. At this stage I would hardly dare to venture an opinion whether in the long term it will amount to a flexible, respected and relatively <u>inexpensive</u> form of regulation, although I think that (except as regards expense) there is a fair chance that it will.

THE SIB/SRO STRUCTURE : ITS ADVANTAGES AND STATE OF HEALTH

Martin J. Vile

I speak to you as a senior executive of the body which neither conceived the Act nor was responsible for its particular terms but which has in effect been given the main responsibility for realising in practice the system envisaged by the Act and for setting the standards of regulation under it, and which can be expected to be held to account for its operation in practice both in terms of investor protection and workability.

It is reasonable to suppose that when the organisers of this seminar decided on the programme they envisaged that if the system of regulation under the Financial Services Act had not been launched the countdown would, at least, be in its final stages. The Government was committed, apparently, to implementation by the end of this year. To achieve that, the last date for firms to apply to Self-regulating Organisations (SROs) or the Securities Investment Board (SIB) to secure the benefit, if necessary, of interim authorisation after entry into force of the Act, would, it was considered, have to be no later than 30th September.

In fact, on 14th September no SRO is recognised. Indeed one indispensable precondition to such a recognition is absent, namely a set of rules which the SIB has formally made under its delegated powers and whose investor protection standards an SRO must meet under the so-called equivalence test.

My paper is therefore about a structure which has yet to be tested in practice, even briefly. And there remains much to accomplish before the Act is fully in force. The

SIB will adopt the bulk of its rule book very shortly, but adoption of, for example, the rules for authorised unit trusts is still some way into the future and the finalisation of a compensation scheme must follow consultations with recognised SROs. The timing of recognition of SROs will depend on the time taken by the Director General of Fair Trading to fulfil his role to advise the Secretary of State on the competition implications of the SROs' rules, but seems unlikely to be completed for some months. Recognised Professional Bodies (RPBs) should be ready to be recognised within a similar time scale.

Recognition of investment exchanges and clearing houses and, consequential on the SIBs' rules, the designation of overseas exchanges is to come; so is designation under the Act by the Secretary of State of countries or territories, for the purposes of the marketing in the United Kingdom, of overseas collective investment schemes and of investment life assurance policies and certification by the Secretary of State of member states of the EEC for the purposes of the authorisation of so-called Europersons operating from the community.

The Government, which is responsible for fixing the relevant dates for entry into force under the Act has recently indicated that it now hopes to bring the regime as a whole into force in early April 1988.

In referring to some - and only some - of the essential building blocks in the creation of the new framework, I have merely hinted at the complexity of the structure now being turned from architect's drawings into institutional reality.

Given the situation as it is now, it is perhaps premature to analyse the structure's "advantages" or, at least without the marvels of the antenatal scanner, its state of health. I would therefore propose to highlight four characteristics of the regulatory framework that have been of particular significance in shaping the nature of the framework:

- the comprehensiveness of its coverage
- the dispersal of responsibilities
- practitioner involvement
- the availability of private remedies in the courts

(1) Comprehensiveness

Inevitably much time and effort is being, and has been devoted by interested parties (not least members of the legal profession) to establishing what the Act and the new framework does not cover - who does not need authorisation; what kinds of activity are not investment business; to what or to whom which rules have been disapplied. Inevitably there are obscurities and anomalies at boundaries of definitions and therefore some surprises as to what is or may be excluded.

One SRO, LAUTRO - the SRO for Life Assurance and Unit Trust producers, has taken the view that they cannot effectively regulate investment business in their area. In effect in their area they have sought to disapply one of the exemptions in the Act. What is much more notable, however, is surely the ambition of the Act in the ground which it seeks to cover.

As referred to by earlier speakers, the requirement for authorisation (or exemption) in section 2 is expressed in very sweeping terms, the list of investments in Part 1 of Schedule 1 is very extensive, the list of activities constituting investment business in Part II of Schedule 1 is very broad, the matters envisaged by the Act to be regulated, cold-calling, clients' money, compensation, conflicts of interest, record-keeping etc. are legion.

The investment business industry in the United Kingdom is very large by any measure and is very diverse. There seem likely to be upwards of 40,000 firms on the register of authorised persons. They include insurance brokers, stockbrokers, futures brokers and commodity brokers;

investment managers and investment advisers; dealers and market-makers in a bewildering variety of very different instruments; wholesalers and retailers; one-man firms and firms with national branch networks; firms such as the Prudential, Merrill Lynch, National Westminster, BZW and the high street solicitor, financial adviser or estate agent. And the tentacles of regulation will spread across the whole country - it is certainly not a matter simply of regulation of the City (or even of the City and Edinburgh).

The pervasiveness and the ambition of the exercise cannot be over-estimated and should be borne in mind by those who question the length of time it is taking for the new framework to become operational. It is exemplified in the size of the SIB rule book, which will be 500 pages, a fact which has also been known to attract critical comment - the length is more a reflection of breadth of subject matter than of a very detailed approach to regulation.

The problems of this comprehensiveness are obvious, particularly at this stage. The difficulty is dealing effectively with the problem in one area without causing unwanted problems in another, developing within the system the necessary expertise and resources, and communicating the need for implications of authorisation to all who may be affected. Its virtue and, in effect its motivation, is that it enables the regulators to aspire to one objective which is shared by both consumers and competitors, namely to treat competitive investment business activities on a broadly consistent basis - hence the degeneration of the "level playing field" into a trite cliché in this area. It also enables the regulators to take into account in framing the regulations the interactions between different parts of the system, for example, between life assurance companies who are the providers as principals of life assurance and collective investment products and the brokers who act as the independent intermediaries of the same products.

(2) Dispersal of Responsibilities

The framework to be established under the Act disperses responsibility vertically and horizontally.

Vertically, some powers will be exercisable only by the Secretary of State, notably prosecution powers and powers involving quasi-diplomatic considerations (e.g. to designate territories for the purpose of the collective investment scheme provisions). Many powers will be exercised by SIB, notably to recognise the other regulatory bodies in the system and to make rules applying to persons whom it authorises, both of which powers, under the overall framework, will set the standard for regulation throughout the system; but a major role will be played in the system by bodies whom SIB recognises - SROs, RPBs, RIEs and RCHs - and who seem likely to bear the brunt of the responsibility for day to day regulation of firms and of investment business.

Horizontally, the regulation of firms seems likely to be dispersed between five SROs and eight RPBs, and between six RIEs and two RCHs so far as exchange transactions are concerned. There will also be what might be described as vicarious regulation by overseas authorities, for example where territories or countries are designated by the Secretary of State, and important roles will be played by the Bank of England, the Department of Trade and Industry, as a regulator of insurance companies, the Building Societies Commission and other regulatory responsibilities that would otherwise have to be fulfilled from the inside.

Such dispersal inevitably risks overlap, duplication, inconsistency, lack of clarity, misunderstandings, matters falling between regulators, lack of co-ordination and so on. The regulators will all have to work very hard to avoid or minimise these dangers and sometimes, no doubt, problems will arise.

But dispersal is, in many ways, a necessary reflection of the scale and diversity of the industry to which I referred earlier. The SROs will have broadly homogeneous memberships distinct from the memberships of other SROs. Firms regulated by RPBs will have more in common with each other and could in theory for the most part have been regulated by an SRO like FIMBRA: but the RPB mechanism enables investment business regulations to be integrated with professional self-regulation and avoids the huge organisational problem and imbalance that an SRO for 35-40,000 intermediaries would have created. And the RIEs will reflect distinct markets. If the principle of self-regulation is to play the part envisaged by the creators of the system, the various regulating units in the self-regulating tier must be ones with which their respective memberships can identify. The fewer the regulators the more difficult would genuine self-regulation be to achieve. The structure will not be static: there may well be convergences between the different SROs or different RIEs in the future, but this will best come spontaneously from the relevant memberships.

(3) Practitioner Involvement

Self-regulation must entail substantial practitioner involvement in regulation - in the direction of the self-regulating bodies and in the formulation and enforcement of their rules. That involvement must certainly be tempered by the involvement of independent persons able through their quality and their numbers to ensure that the public interest - in its broad sense - is adequately taken into account; and the Act imposes a statutory framework that leaves little scope for the self-regulating bodies to become unduly clubbish or inward looking. Given those constraints, self-regulation ought to be informed, practical and up-to-date regulation in a way which even the most sensitive governmental regulation cannot be.

Of course if the standards for regulation are to be set

by SIB, which is not a self-regulating organisation, self-regulation in the lower tier of regulation could be a façade. Hence the importance of the writing into the Act not only that the members of the governing body of SIB must not only be hired and may be fired by the Secretary of State and the Governor of the Bank of England, but that they must include "persons with experience of investment business" as well as "regular users on their own account or on behalf of others of services provided by persons carrying on investment business." As of now, the Board of SIB comprises 10 active practitioners, six non-practitioners, a full-time chairman and the chief executive.

(4) Private Remedies

The novelty of section 62 of the Financial Services Act, under which persons who have suffered loss as a result of breaches of rules may seek a remedy in the courts, may come as a surprise to transatlantic visitors. It is impossible to say to what extent section 62 will be used in practice. Of greater importance may be the power in section 61 for the Secretary of State or the Board to seek a court order for the return of profits which have been made out of, or the remedying of a loss which has been suffered by, an investor on account of breach of the rules.

Predictions of the use of sections 61 and 62 do not really matter. The pertinent fact is that investment businesses are sufficiently concerned about the potential for the use of sections 61 and 62 as to treat them as a major incentive to the securing by them of adequate levels of knowledge of the requirements of the rules within their businesses and of effective compliance with the rules. These particular provisions, perhaps to some extent in their novelty, are therefore having, prospectively, a salutary deterrent effect.

Insofar as advantage is taken of them, they do offer

the prospect for the investor of achieving the making good of what they have suffered, over and above any disciplinary sanctions that may be visited on the erring business.

Conclusion

The system is yet to be in place let along to be tested in action. The magnitude of the operation is huge. The responsibilities on the regulators and the regulated will be very great. There are bound to be teething problems which the system will need to resolve rapidly.

We are, in many ways, now at the point of maximum struggle and unease, the scale of the operation is beginning to be generally appreciated as are the organisational and operational, for example the systems and implications.

The success of the new regulatory framework will depend considerably on the effectiveness in practice of the design and of the tools given to the regulators. But no single design for such a substantial and complex operation could avoid disadvantages as well as advantages. What is likely to count as much as the design is the skill and professionalism of the regulators and the responsiveness and commitment of the regulated: the human factor rather than the legislative.

Leigh Masel

I wanted just to speak about two aspects of Martin Vile's paper in which he mentioned the comprehensiveness of the Act and practitioner involvement.

I thought I would just confine my remarks to those topics. I have some trouble in understanding that this is a true self-regulatory scheme. Classic self-regulation, as it's understood at least in the handbooks, consists of regulation of members of a private organisation and the chief sanction of which is that contravention of the rules brings about, perhaps, a fine, suspension or cancellation of membership of the organisation. The type of legislative framework or regulatory framework which is proposed in the United Kingdom, as I see it, is a sort of disguised licensing framework, where the licensing authority is not the Secretary of State or the Minister but a series of bodies who are themselves authorised by an agency of the Minister, namely SIB, to carry on certain functions and in some cases where the authority would come not from the organisations themselves but from the agency, namely the SIB. And the sanctions which can be applied for infraction of the rules are not simply cancellation or suspension of membership in cases, but the threat of the cancellation of the authority of the so-called self-regulatory organisation reinforced by sanctions in the form of section 62. Now, if I may say so, I do not regard this as a true self-regulatory framework.

There are some things which I think should be applauded e.g. the comprehensiveness of the Act. Now, in my country and I suspect it's the same in the United States and Canada the basic classic regulation is founded upon product, it's a product segmentation. You look at a particular product and you say: is this a security? If it's classified as a security it's regulated in a certain way and persons who advise and deal in securities require to be licensed.

In the case of the United Kingdom scheme, as I understand, regulation is based upon function. That is to say the regulation fastens upon the nature of the business carried on by the intermodiary, and there are a number of products which were listed in Mr. Herrington's paper which would certainly not be required as securities such as long-term insurance bonds. Each Monday morning, many Australian investors open up their Australian Financial Review to see how their collective investments are getting along and on one page, under the heading of Trusts and Funds Markets, there are listed the various equity trusts with their respective buy-back and purchase figures and under a separate heading the buy-back and purchase figures for insurance bonds. This appearance of commonality between the two types of funds, namely the equity trusts on the one hand and the insurance bonds on the other, in reality disguises the world of difference in the regulatory structure in Australia. Equity trusts are regarded, in law, as securities because they come within the definition of prescribed interests and as such are regulated by the Securities Industry Act and by the Companies Code. Insurance bonds answer the description of life insurance policies and as life assurance policies they are expressly exempted from the definition of prescribed interests and therefore are not regulated as securities.

So it seems somewhat strange to many people that a salesman who sells both interests in equity trusts and insurance bonds is not required to be licensed under the Securities Acts if he sells interests in trusts. I think one of the benefits of the United Kingdom scheme is that the difference which has been so fundamentally a classic regulation in North American and Australia is eliminated.

Now, I am somewhat sceptical about the aspect of practitioner involvement. In my view there are some assumptions which I think should be closely examined. In Australia, opinions differ as to the viability of existing professional organisations within the securities industry to assume formalised self-regulatory roles and the arguments for and against self-regularisation are neatly incapsulated in a Green Paper published in 1985 which reviewed the licensing provisions of the Securities Act and Code and made some recommendations for reform relating to the licensing of securities industry participation.

My main concern is that very few self-regulatory organisations have the resources to establish and maintain programmes which involve advertising codes, improved disclosure and information standards, enhancement of prospectus and trust deed forms, drafting of guide lines for avoidance of possible conflicts of interests development and know your clients standards, and all those other matters which are intended to lift standards and result in improved perceptions for operation in the industry.

If the structure of stock exchanges can be regarded as a criteria, I would say that the stock exchanges were devised for a different era. Stock exchanges were geared to maintain benefits which would now be regarded as monopolistic for their members in return for the acceptance of restrictions by members on why, when, how, where and what charges they made for transacting business. Manifestations of this policy, now happily abandoned in Australia, were fixed rates of brokerage, natural person membership, supported by a restrictive system of election to membership, limitations on advertising and prohibition of membership by a person of more than one state's stock exchanges. All of this was designed to protect existing firms. All that has been done in the wake of the Trade Practices Commission and the wave of new technology, and in fact, as of April of this year, the Australian Stock Exchange was established which in effect became the holding company for the six stock exchanges in the capital cities, and natural and corporate members of the six capital cities are now members of the ASX, as its called.

The exclusivity which was the object of the original exchanges is not the main challenge today. Certainly, the main challenge in Australia is for the ASX and each of its subsidiaries to ensure that major markets in securities issued by Australia's top 50 securities remains in Australia. Trading in these securities represents over 70% of the value of all stocks and equities reported on the Australian exchanges and if that market moves substantially to London and/or New York the larger member organisations in Australia will be compelled to join exchanges in those cities in order to remain in business.

Today the priorities of Australian stock exchanges are not so much maintenance or disciplines over members but the desire to ensure such facilities as a low transactional cost national market, available for trading 24 hours a day if necessary, efficient information services an efficient delivery and settlement systems which will guarantee completion of contract by Australian brokers and a central market facility which concentrates the order of flow sufficiently to maintain liquidity and accuracy of the present system are available.

It's doubtful whether a stock exchange today can represent itself as a professional organisation representing solely stock brokers. The reality is that member organisations can be owned 100% by non-members. And the task before the Australian stock exchanges, if I can use Australia as a criterion, is to manage the exchanges' substantial assets and to have staff which require knowledge, skill and experience for the task.

The skills required to run a stock exchange are not necessarily the skills required of good stock brokers. With emphasis on competition in the broking industry and competition between markets located in principal capital cities, it's unlikely that members would have the time or inclination to administer the day to day activities of the exchanges. The management of stock exchanges has become increasingly more technical due to deregulation, advances in technology and pressures from investment facilities outside the stock exchanges. Members of committees of a stock exchange would like to be involved almost exclusively as policy makers and this can only be achieved by the employment of sufficiently skilled staff able to carry out the normal responsibilities of senior management.

My point is a simple one, the classic self-regulation, particularly with the formulation of business conduct, codes of ethics and disciplines of members to say nothing of training and education may very well constitute a low priority in the programme of so-called self-regulatory organisations.

If what I have said about stock exchanges is extended to other self-regulatory organisations involved in the investment business, the dream of self-regulation as envisaged in the United Kingdom may yet prove to be a façade.

Peter Dey

There are two aspects of the Big Bang which are the focus of this seminar. One is the deregulation of the rules concerning access to the capital markets, and the second is the creation of the statutory scheme which combines both the public and private regulatory scheme of regulation.

Now the first aspect of Big Bang is comparable to the reforms of the rules in Canada concerning access to the capital markets which really is the full extent of our big bang. But the second aspect of the UK Big Bang represents for us an ambition of staggering proportions when we consider that it has taken us some six or seven decades to achieve a scheme of securities regulation which is, not surprisingly, still subject to extensive, constant and regular reform.

Now it's the second aspect which has already been discussed in the papers. I would like to make a couple of general observations concerning the UK and Canadian schemes. By way of opening, it's apparent that the UK scheme contains all the elements of securities regulation with which we, in Canada, are familiar. For example, there is a licensing requirement for the market intermediaries, there are disclosure requirements imposed upon those seeking to raise capital from the securities markets, there is the comprehensive scheme regulating tender offers, take-over bids, there is a system of sanctions applicable for those who don't comply with the rules and on top of this there is a public regulatory authority that oversees the activities of the self-regulatory organisations as well as administers the comprehensive scheme of regulation.

There are three significant aspects of the SIB structure that I would like to comment upon. First, is the structure of the regulatory bodies. Our public authority is a securities commission which is both an administrative body and a judicial body. As an administrative body it licences intermediaries, it clears prospectuses, conducts investigations of complaints and so on. As a judicial body it has the power to cease trade activities in the market place, deny access to the markets and so on. The structural issue for us is whether one body can effectively wear two hats at the same time - both a judicial hat and an administrative hat. Can the commission act to cease trading a particular transaction when its staff is one of the parties appearing for it? It would appear that the SIB, if it decides to proceed against a bad apple in the market place, is encouraged to do so under the UK scheme before the courts and therefore it will have the same status in the sanctioning process as the person that is alleged to have transgressed the rules. It is not both the judge and the prosecutor, and as our securities commission becomes more interventionist I think the "dual capacity" of our securities regulator will be an increasingly important issue.

The second aspect of the structure upon which I would like to comment is the discretion exercised by the regulatory authority. In our Canadian scheme of regulation, the commission has discretion to cease trade any activity in the market place. It can deny access in the market place for new issues, it can deny access to markets to any person or company, it can grant exemptions from the scheme of regulation and so on. The importance of these discretionary powers is that they are not just exercisable in the event that somebody doesn't comply with the rules but they are exercisable in pursuit of the public interest and that is a very vague and subjective standard for exercising some very heavy powers. Indeed our statute could have been a very brief statute if it had been drafted to reflect the reality and that is really that the power to regulate is vested in this authority and this authority really assumes to itself the power to prescribe the rules through its exercise of discretion in the public interest. Now whether a scheme of securities regulation is more or less restrictive than another scheme of regulation really depends in many respects on the extent of the discretion and the manner in which the discretion apparent in the scheme is exercised. Broad discretion seems to be part of every system of securities regulation that is necessary because of the dynamic nature of the market place and the inability of the law makers to anticipate all of the issues that can arise in the market place, but I guess I would like to applaud the UK structure which appears to direct the exercise of judicial powers to the courts away from the securities regulatory authorities.

The extent of the discretion exercised by the securities regulatory authorities, I think, is also a function of the private remedies available. What we have discovered is that the extent of government intervention in the market place is really a function of the militancy of the investment community in redressing what it regards as oppressive conduct by corporate managers. In our jurisdiction, the investment community has historically been heavily dependent upon the government regulator to intervene to protect their rights and because of this our scheme might be characterised as more restrictive than the scheme that is being anticipated in the United Kingdom. However, the trend in Canada is for investors and share holders to be better organised and to muster their war chests to take on the corporate managers. The result of course is that the regulator need not be so interventional and I think this improves the credibility of the process if the substantive rights that are involved in the conflicts take place in the market place rather than in some defective process before the administrative tribunal.

Now the third and final aspect of the regulatory structure upon which I would like to comment is the relationship between the public authority and the self-regulatory authorities. When I was at the Securities Commission in Ontario I became a very strong believer in self-regulation but I also came to believe that the survival of a scheme of self-regulation depended heavily upon the involvement of a public authority overseeing the activities of the self-regulators. The oversight is really quite passive in our experience but it assures the public market place that the SRO is not a private combine created to gouge the public and it assures the public that the existence of the public authority overseeing the self-regulatory authority is a constraint upon excessive self-regulation which might be used by the members of the SRO to effectively reduce competition.

It is my impression that a comparable relationship exists between the SIB and the SROs in the United Kingdom and I think it's an important element of the scheme of securities regulation that is contemplated in the United Kingdom and I think in many respects it will ensure the longevity of the SROs.

<u>Al Sommer</u>

As I read the <u>Economist</u> and the London <u>Financial Times</u> and some of the other publications that cross my desk, I get the impression that the controversy over the new system of regulation in the United Kingdom is far from resolved and that there may even be some people who think that maybe an SEC wouldn't have been a bad idea after all. Now that's a form of heresy, I suppose, in this country but I noticed a subtle change in the <u>Economist</u> where three or four years ago the theme was: save us from the SEC. Now I think there is a subtle note creeping in there that maybe it isn't as bad as we once thought given what has been offered to us as a substitute. I would remark on a couple of details and one is that Leigh Masel discusses the breadth of this legislation and scheme with regard to the definition of securities. If you really want to learn something about the breadth of that meaning you should read the cases which have arisen under the definition of investment contract in American Law. Another detail, before I get into broader comments is that any scheme that contemplates the possibility of regulating lawyers under securities law gives American lawyers the shivers. We have enough trouble with the SEC as it is where they have no such explicit authority so this is an element which I hope is not translated 3,500 miles to the West.

It seems to be that one of the great pieces of good judgment that was exercised in the United Kingdom was the avoidance of something like May Day. By calling it Big Bang I think it had far less an ominous tone than the nickname that was given to the elimination of fixed commissions in the United States which we improvidently fixed for 1st May, which did two things. One, it suggested that maybe we were communists because the communists celebrate on 1st May and the second thing was that it gave the excuse for people regarding this as some sort of emergency situation so that May Day became some sort of a terminal programme.

I admire the British in undertaking such a comprehensive change in their scheme of regulations at a time when there are such tremendous changes going on in the way in which securities are traded in this country and elsewhere. There is the multiplication of the number of private shareholders in this country, there is the intensification of competition among markets for parts of the global business, there is the proliferation of products and ways of doing business and I think it's extremely courageous in the midst of all this to impose such a radically, new and different scheme of regulation. I could compare to the United States endlessly but I'm going to confine myself to just a few general remarks. First of all I think the American system is based upon the Manichean concept of human nature. I think it expresses a certain suspicion that people are inclined to engage in this conduct and we must to watch them pretty carefully.On the other hand, I see the British system as more passive perhaps and believes in the unique goodness of man. That sort of judgment is justified by a quotation from the White Paper published in January 1985 - in dealing with the problem of providing information to experts the paper said there were two possible ways of proceeding: this category of people could be defined in statute and approach adopted by the regulatory laws of the United States of America. The other approach is to follow good, British market practice and rely on discretion and common sense and perhaps that summarises more than anything the difference of approach being taken. It seems to me that, putting it in a nutshell, the role of SROs in the United States is basically that they are a part of the system. In the British system I think they are the heart of the system.

I think that if the SROs under the scheme that has been developed in the United Kingdom, did their job and did as they are expected to do in every respect I suspect that there would be relatively little for the SIB to do. On the other hand if the self-regulatory organisations in the United States did their jobs with equal competence and comprehensiveness I suspect the SEC would still employ 2,000 people, spend $120m and have a lot to do. There is a very basic difference because under the American scheme the SEC has jurisdiction over a number of matters that cannot be delegated to the SROs. Just as an example, registration statements for public offerings of securities both initial public offerings and subsequent ones all have to go through the SEC. You cannot delegate that to the exchanges. The same thing with a system of continuous disclosure which is administered with the SEC and cannot be delegated. A large part of the regulation of investment companies, investment advisors must be done by the SEC and could not be delegated to anyone else. There is a good deal of regulation of broker dealers that is unintelligible and of course there is a very active enforcement programme that I suspect the SEC would be reluctant to cede to anyone, self-regulatory or not.

I think there are lot of good things about the UK system that are developing - certain logical consistency, it's comprehensive, the lines of authority seem to run with skill and consistency, you have the Parliament, the DTI, the SIB, the SROs and all the rest of it and it all seems to hang together very neatly. There is obviously an enlargement of the role of the Government in the oversight of the SROs and as Leigh Masel said, maybe they are not SROs any more. A suspicion has existed in the United States with regard to our SROs that maybe they are no longer SROs, particularly since the 1985 amendments. There are a lot of good things - there is an explicit statutory recognition that all investors are not created as equal or as smart or as informed as all other investors. That is a realisation that we have come to only recently in the United States and we have implemented pretty much by rule, regulation and interpretation with very little assistance from the statutes.

Now, where are the problems that I see in this? I guess, if you look at my background and my predilections, I think one of the absolute essentials of any system of securities regulation is good, solid, tough enforcement and obviously the SEC has a certain pride in the fact that they are that. As I look at this scheme I find that the enforcement methods, the enforcement powers are dispersed - some of them are going to be in the prosecutors, some of them are going to be in the DTI, some are going to be in the SIB, some of them are going to be in the SROs, some are going to be in private hands - the private clause of action. That is not bad because there is a certain dispersion of that in the United States as well. Central to the enforcement effort in the United States is the SEC and I think that all of you have read of the investigations that have gone on with regard to insider trading, while those that have claimed the headlines, there is still an ongoing programme of enforcement with regard to a lot of other areas of conduct affecting securities in the United States.

It seems to me that the test is going to be whether indeed there is going to be effective, good enforcement and whether the SROs and the SIB are going to have enforcement-minded people somewhere within their structure. Now there is a great deal of uncertainty being expressed in this country about the whole scheme, a lot of uneasiness, a lot of criticism of it. Let me say this, it seems to me that all of that is premature. I am a sceptic. When we eliminated fixed commissions in the United States I remember all the predictions of gloom, doom and destruction that came upon us, I remember distinctly one meeting at which the head of one of the largest and most prosperous securities firms in the United States, one that I might add has continued to prosper, got up at the meeting, pointed his finger at me and said: "Commissioner Sommer, if you and your colleagues persist in this course of action you will not only destroy the securities industry in this country you will undermine the base of capitalism in the western world". At that I looked over my shoulder to see who, in heavens name, he was talking about because they didn't tell me I had that kind of power. But in any event there seems to be a rough ratio that if you take in order of 1 to 10 the expectations are about 10 times as bad as the reality turns out to be. So I don't put a great deal of store into what I hear about the terrible things that are likely to happen under this system. Every time in the United States, in my experience, when they have introduced a new wrinkle in regulation it has always been accompanied by fear, gloom and desperation. If you read back the history of the 1933 and 1934 Acts, they were going to destroy the securities industry and there would never be another underwriting in the United States. The whole system was going to hell in a hand basket because of these terrible regulators in Washington. We all know those things didn't come true thank heaven.

Confusion and uncertainty at the onset of a regulatory scheme in my estimation are inevitable. You cannot write statutes, you cannot write rules that are so crystalline and so clear and so easily perceived that there are not going to be ambiguities at the edge of them, that there aren't going to be problems that have to be resolved. After 50 years of regulation in the United States we are still in the process of defining what is a security. So the confusions are not going to be eliminated immediately, it takes time to do them and I am confident that in time that will be done.

In the final analysis, in my estimation, it is not the system that tells the story, it's how the system is administered. If it is administered by people who have imagination, who have flexibility, who are quick to recognise the places where you need a little sandpaper, where you need a little carving off of the edges, if it is administered by people who have a determination to make it work and if it is administered, in some part, by people who believe that there are bad people selling securities and engaging in various activities related to securities and if that those bad people should be punished, then I think the system will work.

NEW ISSUES: THE LEGAL FRAMEWORK FOR PROSPECTUS APPROVAL AND THE PROFESSIONAL EXEMPTION FOR THE EURODOLLAR MARKET

Ralph Aldwinckle

1. Introduction

As a result of the Financial Services Act we are in the process of going through what is probably the most radical revision of prospectus law which has ever taken place in this country. It would be nice to report that this all resulted from a well-conceived plan which had been the subject of informed public debate, but I cannot do this. The truth is that the White Paper, which preceded the Financial Services Bill, was studiously vague to the point of incomprehensibility about its proposals for prospectus law. In any event the provisions which appeared in the Bill were substantially rewritten in the course of the Bill's progress through Parliament. Some of the more significant concepts embodied in the Act were developed almost by accident, having been taken from EEC Directives negotiated in the 1970s, at a time when no thought had been given by the Commission, much less the UK Government, that they might one day, form the basis for UK prospectus law.

It would also be nice if I could give a clear summary of what the new regime will consist of when fully implemented. But without a crystal ball I cannot. Both in relation to Part V of the Act and in relation to the rules about investment advertisements (section 57) the picture is still unclear. This is because in both areas the Act provides only a framework: much of the detail is to be filled in by secondary legislation. At present we have only the most general idea of what that detail will cover.

2. The Relationship between Parts IV and V

Under previous Companies Acts prospectus law applied in the same way to listed securities as it did to unlisted securities. But the Financial Services Act continues a distinction, first introduced by the Stock Exchange (Listing) Regulations 1984, between the two types. Part IV deals with listed securities, Part V with unlisted.

"Listed" in this context means admitted to official listing on the Stock Exchange, in London. "Unlisted" means anything else. So a share listed on the New York or Luxembourg Stock Exchanges, or a share dealt in on the (London) Stock Exchange's own Unlisted Securities Market, is "unlisted".

Part IV covers not only the whole process by which securities are admitted to official listing but also the obligations to which issuers are subject once they have obtained listing. Part V is more limited. It is principally concerned with the requirements for prospectuses in relation to unlisted securities.

There are some provisions which are more or less the same in both Parts IV and V. The most important are those which have to do with liability for listing particulars or prospectuses. I shall come back to these after I have compared the other provisions of the two Parts.

3. Part IV

(1) The Background

The basis of Part IV is three EEC Directives: the Admission Directive which was adopted in 1979, the Listing Particulars Directive which was adopted in 1980 and the Interim Reports Directive which was adopted in 1982.

These Directives are intended to harmonise the minimum requirements in relation to listing while leaving member states, or their competent authorities, free to impose what the Directives call "more stringent or additional requirements". These were initially implemented by the 1984 Listing Regulations which made the Directives, as they stood, directly part of UK law. The "more stringent or additional" requirements over and above the minimum requirements of the Directives were left, as before, to the Stock Exchange itself.

(2) The Structure

Under the new regime in Part IV some of the provisions of the Directives are embodied in Part IV and as such represent part of UK statutory law, as was the case with the Listing Regulations. However, the bulk of the requirements of the Directives are neither contained in Part IV nor imposed directly on issuers. Instead the Council of the Stock Exchange, as competent authority, is given power to make listing rules. It is under no statutory duty to comply with the Directives in drawing up those rules. However, section 192 gives the Secretary of State the power to give directions to the Council if it appears to him that it would otherwise contravene the requirements of the Directives. Thus, observance of the Directives is ensured, but in a less direct way.

(3) Listing Rules "in Accordance with Part IV"

The statutory power to make listing rules applies not only to the minimum requirements of the Directives but also to the Stock Exchange's own "more stringent or additional" requirements. The source of such rules has therefore become a statutory one. As a result the bulk of the Stock Exchange's rules (The Yellow Book) represents listing rules for the purposes of Part IV. However, there are some issuers and securities which are outside Part IV. Part IV makes it clear that these can still be listed under the Stock Exchange's own rules.

(4) The Types of Security to which Part IV Applies

Part IV applies only to certain types of investments defined by the Financial Services Act. Roughly speaking it applies to shares, debt securities, warrants to subscribe (although not to purchase) shares and various types of depository receipt in respect of shares. Although shares in building societies, industrial and provident societies or credit unions are not investments for other purposes of the Act, they are caught by Part IV. Debt securities issued by states are included unless they are issued by an EEC member state or a local authority in such a member state. Appendix 1 sets out the relevant part of Schedule 1 to the Act showing how it applies in relation to Part IV.

In addition the Secretary of State has power to extend Part IV so as to apply to units in a collective investment scheme. These include such obvious things as unit trusts, but they also include shares in open-ended investment companies and closed-ended unit trusts.

(5) Listing Particulars

Contents

Part IV leaves the content of listing particulars almost entirely to the listing rules. However, it does restate Article 4(1) of the Listing Particulars Directive which contains the duty to include all information necessary to enable investors and their investment advisers to make an informed assessment of the securities in question.

The Act clarifies two important points as compared with the Directive. First, the information required is that which is within the knowledge of the person responsible or which it would be reasonable for him to obtain by making enquiries. Secondly, in deciding what information is material, one may have regard to information already published either as a result of statutory requirements e.g. annual accounts or as a result of the listing rules e.g. previous listing particulars etc.

Derogation

In certain circumstances the competent authority has power to grant derogations from this general duty. The first two (public interest and detriment to the issuer) are taken from Article 7 of the Listing Particulars Directive, whilst the third is to clarify an apparent conflict in the Directive and to make it clear that in those cases where the competent authority has power to relax the detailed requirements of the Directive (the main example being Article X of the Directive) issuers are not required to reinstate those detailed items as a result of the general duty.

Registration

Listing particulars have to be registered with the Companies Registry. That was already the position under the Listing Regulations, but Part IV has gone one step further and requires supplementary listing particulars also to be registered.

(6) Supplementary Listing Particulars

When are they required?

Supplementary listing particulars are required if before the start of dealings there is a significant change affecting any matter in the listing particulars, or a significant matter arises which would have had to be included if it had arisen when the particulars were prepared. For this purpose "significant" means something which is significant for the purpose of making an informed assessment of the matters required under the general duty.

Duty to publish

The issuer has to submit them to the competent authority and, subject to their being approved, publish them. This duty of publication is not placed on other persons responsible for the particulars, but if they become aware of a significant change or a significant new matter they are under a duty to notify the issuer. Failure by the issuer to publish or by a person responsible to notify carries liability.

4. The Regime under Part V

(1) The Structure

As I have already explained Part V is more limited in its effects than Part IV in that it is almost entirely concerned with prospectuses in relation to an issue or an offering of "unlisted securities" i.e. anything which is not admitted to full listing under Part IV.

Part V represents only a framework because the Secretary of State has power to make rules regarding a variety of things including exemptions in relation to primary and secondary offers, and the information which prospectuses must contain.

None of those regulations have been published in draft, so at this stage the practical implications of Part V are very difficult to discern.

(2) The Types of Security to which Part V Applies

The securities to which Part V applies are very much the same as those to which Part IV applies, but securities issued by a government, local authority or public authority are entirely outside Part V whether or not the government etc. is within the EEC, as are shares in building societies, industrial and provident societies or credit unions. Appendix 2 sets out the relevant part of Schedule 1 to the Act showing how it applies to Part V.

(3) When is a Prospectus Required?

<u>"An advertisement offering securities"</u>

The Companies Act definition of a prospectus is an offer or invitation to the public to subscribe or purchase securities. As a result it does not apply where securities are offered by way of exchange, the most obvious example being a paper for paper take-over offer. Under Part V the result is different and such an offer will potentially be caught. However, Part V goes further and applies not only to an offer or invitation to acquire securities but also to a document containing information "calculated to lead directly or indirectly to a person entering into an agreement to acquire securities". It also catches underwriting.

<u>The types of offer</u>

There are three circumstances under which a prospectus may be required:

(a) an offer of securities on the occasion of their admission to dealings on an approved recognised investment exchange ("an ARIE") or on terms that they will be issued if admitted to such dealings;

(b) a primary offer; or

(c) a secondary offer.

A primary offer is an advertisement offering securities issued otherwise than on admission to an ARIE, where the agreement which is to be entered into is one to subscribe or to underwrite securities i.e. an invitation to purchase existing securities is excluded.

A secondary offer is an offer issued other than on admission to an ARIE where the agreement invited is to acquire, rather than to subscribe or underwrite, securities and the advertisement is issued or caused to be issued by:

(a) a person who acquired the securities from the issuer with a view to issuing such an advertisement in respect of them; or

(b) a person who, with a view to issuing such advertisement in respect of them, has acquired the securities other than from the issuer but without their having been admitted to dealings on an ARIE or held by a person who acquired them as an investment, and without any intention that such an advertisement should be issued in respect of them; or

(c) a person who is a controller of the issuer or has been a controller in the previous 12 months and is acting with the consent or participation of the issuer in issuing the advertisement.

(4) Exemptions from Requirement to File Prospectus

The exemptions are summarised in Appendix 3. No filing is required in the following cases:

Exemptions applicable in all three cases

(a) The advertisement is such that no agreement can be entered into in pursuance of it until a prospectus has been delivered (section 159(1)(b) and 160(1)(b));

(b) the offer is conditional on admission to listing under Part IV (section 161(1));

(c) other securities issued by the same issuer are dealt in on an ARIE and the ARIE certifies that sufficient information is available to investors (section 161(3));

(d) the advertisement falls within section 58(2) (a special class of advertisement giving limited information) (section 161(2)); or

(e) if an order is made by the Secretary of State in cases where foreign law provides equivalent protection (section 161(4)).

Exemptions applicable both to primary and secondary offers

The Secretary of State may make regulations exempting advertisements:

(a) having a private character;

(b) dealing with investments only incidentally;

(c) issued to persons sufficiently expert to understand any risks;

(d) relating to investments of a kind normally bought or dealt in by persons sufficiently expert to understand any risks; or

(e) of any other classes;

(sections 160(6) and (7)).

It is under these powers that the all-important Eurobond exemptions will be made.

<u>Exemptions applicable only in the case of offers on admission to an ARIE</u>

(a) Where a prospectus has been filed in the previous 12 months and the ARIE certifies that sufficient information is available to investors (section 161(1)); or

(b) where the securities have been listed in accordance with Part IV in the previous 12 months and the ARIE gives a similar certificate (section 159(2)).

<u>Exemptions applicable only in the case of secondary offers</u>

Where a prospectus has been filed in the past six months in respect of a primary or secondary offer of those securities.

(5) Contents

<u>Detailed contents</u>

These will be prescribed by statutory instrument. However, in the case of some ARIEs (e.g. it is hoped, the Stock Exchange in relation to the Unlisted Securities Market) the rules of the ARIE will be permitted by the Secretary of State to apply instead of the statutory rules.

General duty

The general duty is in more or less the same terms as in Part IV and an ARIE permitted to do so by the Secretary of State has similar powers to allow derogations from the general duty.

(6) Supplementary Prospectuses

Again, Part V follows Part IV in requiring a supplementary prospectus in certain circumstances.

5. Liability

(1) Relationship of Parts IV and V

Parts IV and V are substantially the same in this context. Each Part contains sections establishing liability to pay compensation for false or misleading statements, exemptions from liability to pay compensation and detailed provisions as to the persons responsible. However, neither has any effect on liabilities arising in contract or tort: those continue to exist independently.

(2) Criminal Liability

As with the Listing Regulations, but in contrast to the Companies Act, the Act provides no specific criminal liability for misstatements in listing particulars. Instead the general offence in section 47(1) relating to misstatements made dishonestly or recklessly will apply.

(3) Civil Liability

Sections 150 and 166 say that the persons responsible for any listing particulars or prospectus or supplement are liable to pay compensation to any person who has

(a) acquired any of the securities in question; and

(b) suffered loss in respect of them as a result of any untrue or misleading statement in the particulars or prospectus or the omission from them of any matter required to be included under

  (i) the general duty of disclosure or
  (ii) the duty to publish supplementary listing particulars or a supplementary prospectus.

As with the Listing Regulations, but in contrast to the Companies Act, there is no need to show reliance on the misstatement. All that is necessary is for the loss to have resulted from the misstatement.

Misstatement for this purpose includes an omission but only insofar as the information in question was required under the general duty to include all material information or under the duty to publish a supplement to the listing particulars or prospectus. So, the mere omission of a detailed item of information required by the relevant rules will not, of itself, lead to liability.

Unlike the Companies Act where only a subscriber can sue, a subsequent purchaser in the market can sue. There is no time limit for this purpose. All that one can say is that the longer the time that goes by the less likely it is that the loss can be shown to have been caused by the misstatement.

(4) Who is Liable? - Persons Responsible

<u>The definition</u>

Sections 152 and 168 define what is meant by the "persons responsible". They are:

(a) the issuer of the securities;

(b) its directors;

(c) each person who has authorised himself to be named, and is named, as having agreed to become a director of the issuer. It is common in recommended take-over offers to state, for example, that the chairman of the offeree will join the board of the offeror on the offer becoming unconditional. Under both Parts IV and V he will thereby become responsible for the information concerning the offeror, as well, of course, as that concerning his own company;

(d) "each person who accepts, and is stated in the particulars as accepting, responsibility for, or for any part, of the particulars". This means, in effect, anyone who gives the responsibility statement required by the Stock Exchange's Yellow Book; and

(e) "each person not falling within any of the foregoing [categories] who has authorised the contents of, or any part of, the particulars".

There are a variety of problems as to what (e) means.

Persons responsible for part

Under sections 152(3) and 168(3) if someone who falls within heading (d) or (e) has accepted responsibility for, or authorised only part of the particulars he is responsible only for that part. So on a recommended take-over, where the offeree's directors accept responsibility for the information relating to their company, that is all that they will be responsible for.

Section 152(4) goes on to deal with the other side of

the coin and to say, in effect, that in that situation the offeror's directors are not responsible for the information regarding the offeree.

Director in a position of conflict

It sometimes happens that, for example, a director of the offeror is also a director of the offeree. Sections 152(5) and 168(5), in effect, give the Stock Exchange power to permit him to abstain from the document and not be a "person responsible". This power applies whenever "by reason of his having an interest or of any other circumstances" it is "inappropriate" for him to be responsible.

Eurobond issues

Section 153(5) also, in effect, allows the continuation of the practice of corporate responsibility statements in the case of London listed issues of Eurobonds.

(5) Defences

The defences to liability are as follows:

Publication without knowledge etc.

A person is not liable if the particulars or prospectus were published without his knowledge or consent and on becoming aware of publication he gives reasonable public notice.

Part not included in form and context

A person who is responsible for part only of the particulars or prospectus is not liable if the part is not included in (or substantially in) the form and context to which he has agreed.

Reasonable belief

A person is not liable if he shows that at the time when the particulars were submitted to the Stock Exchange or the prospectus was filed he "reasonably believed, having made all such enquiries (if any) as were reasonable, that the statement was true and not misleading or that the matter whose omission caused the loss was properly omitted". However, he must, in addition, show that one of four further conditions has been fulfilled, namely that:

(a) he continued in that belief until the securities were acquired;

(b) they were acquired before it was reasonably practicable to bring a correction to the attention of those likely to acquire them;

(c) before the securities were acquired, he had taken all reasonable steps to secure that a correction was brought to the attention of such persons; or

(d) he continued in that belief until after commencement of dealings and the securities were acquired after such a lapse of time that he ought reasonably to be excused.

Experts' statements

It is a defence to show that, at the time the particulars were submitted to the Stock Exchange or the prospectus was filed, the person responsible believed, on reasonable grounds, that the expert was competent to make or authorise the statement and had consented to its inclusion in the form and context in which it was included. Here again four additional conditions have to be fulfilled. They are equivalent to those I have already mentioned.

<u>Correction</u>

Even if reasonable belief cannot be proved, there is still a defence if the person responsible can show that:

(a) before the securities were acquired a correction was suitably published; or

(b) he took all reasonable steps to secure such publication and reasonably believed that it had taken place before the securities were acquired.

<u>Statement by official, or in public document</u>

It is a defence to show that the statement concerned is an accurate and fair reproduction of a statement made by an official person or contained in an official public document.

<u>Plaintiff knew of misstatement or omission</u>

It is a defence to show that the person suffering the loss acquired the securities with knowledge that the statement was false or misleading or of the omitted matter (or, in the case of supplementary listing particulars, the change or new matter).

(6) How is Liability to be Shared?

As is obvious, it is likely that there may be several people who are responsible for particulars or prospectuses and are therefore liable to investors. The question of how such loss is shared between them is not dealt with by the Act. However, the Civil Liability (Contribution) Act 1978 would normally apply.

(7) What Loss?

The compensation extends to loss in respect of the securities in question as a result of any misrepresentation. Thus, it seems that the question which needs to be asked is: what is the difference between the value of the securities had the representation been true and the value of the securities in the light of the misrepresentation? Thus stated, the proposition is quite straightforward. It is much more difficult to apply in practice and it is likely to be some considerable time before the position is clarified.

6. Investment Advertisements

Section 57 of the Act contains rules about "investment advertisements", which are widely defined.

Listing particulars and prospectuses are "investment advertisements", but under section 58 there are exemptions which allow them to be distributed although in the case of prospectuses relating to non-cash issues where the securities are not dealt in on an ARIE the exemption does not apply.

However, other documents are circulated in relation to issues such as offering telexes on a Eurobond issue. Most of these will be "investment advertisements". If they are not exempted the only way in which they can be issued is either by, or with the approval of, an authorised person, and under the SIB's rules authorised persons are restricted as to the circumstances under which they may issue or approve such advertisements. Also, as indicated above, in relation to Part V an "investment advertisement" may in addition be "an advertisement offering securities" thus making registration of a prospectus necessary unless one of the exemptions applies.

Section 58(3) contains powers for exemptions to be made

by secondary legislation in cases similar to those referred to under the subheading 'Exemptions applicable to both primary and secondary offers'.

7. Eurobonds

(1) London Listed Issues

The Financial Services Act has not made any great change in practice because the three EEC Directives had already been implemented by the Stock Exchange (Listing) Regulations 1984. Under Article X of the Listing Particulars Directive the competent authority may make derogations for Eurobond issues and has done so, although its scope in relation to convertible issues is limited. What remains uncertain is what the exemptions in relation to investment advertisements will be, but it is to be hoped that they will not upset the present position.

(2) Other Issues

Here it is hoped that the exemptions will allow Eurobonds to be exempt both from the requirements in relation to the filing of prospectuses and in relation to investment advertisements, thus continuing the effect (although in a different context) of the combined exemptions in the Companies Act 1985 and the Prevention of Fraud (Investments) Act 1958.

8. Conclusions

In relation to Part V and investment advertisements it is premature to draw any conclusions: too much depends on what the regulations are to say. However, particularly in relation to secondary offers there are potential problems. Also there are considerable problems, both in that context and in the context of investment advertisements, with screen-based information. It is unclear how (or whether) those problems will be dealt with in such a way as to produce a satisfactory solution.

Even then, there is further upheaval on the horizon. The EEC Commission has been pressing ahead in recent months with the draft Prospectus Directive which had been put into limbo some years ago, many hoping that it would never be revived. The efforts of the International Primary Markets Association were instrumental in stopping it being adopted earlier this year in a form which would have done immense damage to the Euromarkets. However, the Commission is still proceeding and it is vital that what emerges represents a practicable and workable solution.

Appendix 1

Paragraphs 1 to 5 of Schedule 1 restated to reflect Part IV modifications (Section 142(3))

Shares etc.

1. Shares and stock in the share capital of a company.

Note. In this paragraph "company" includes any body corporate and also any unincorporated body constituted under the law of a country or territory outside the United Kingdom but does not include an open-ended investment company.

Debentures

2. Debentures, including debenture stock, loan stock, bonds, certificates of deposit and other instrument creating or acknowledging indebtedness, not being instruments issued by the government of a member state or a local authority in a member state.

Note. This paragraph shall not be construed as applying:

(a) to any instrument acknowledging or creating indebtedness for, or for money borrowed to defray, the consideration payable under a contract for the supply of goods or services;

(b) to a cheque or other bill of exchange, a banker's draft or a letter of credit; or

(c) to a banknote, a statement showing a balance in a current, deposit or savings account or (by reason of any financial obligation contained in it) to a lease or other disposition of property, a heritable security or an insurance policy.

3. [omitted]

Instruments entitling to shares or securities

4. Warrants or other instruments entitling the holder to subscribe for investments falling within paragraph 1 above.

Note.

(1) It is immaterial whether the investments are for the time being in existence or identifiable.

(2) An investment falling within this paragraph shall not be regarded as falling within paragraph 7, 8 or 9 below.

Certificates representing securities

5. Certificates or other instruments which confer:

(a) property rights in respect of any investment falling within paragraph 1 above;

(b) any right to acquire, dispose of, underwrite or convert such an investment, being a right to which the holder would be entitled if he held any such investment to which the certificate or instrument relates; or

(c) a contractual right (other than an option) to acquire any such investment otherwise than by subscription.

Note. This paragraph does not apply to any instrument which confers rights in respect of two or more investments issued by different persons.

Appendix 2

Paragraphs 1 to 5 of Schedule 1 restated to reflect Part V modifications (Section 158(2))

Shares etc.

1. Shares and stock in the share capital of a company.

Note. In this paragraph "company" includes any body corporate and also any unincorporated body constituted under the law of a country or territory outside the United Kingdom but does not include an open-ended investment company or any body incorporated under the law of, or any part of, the United Kingdom relating to building societies, industrial and provident societies or credit unions.

Debentures

2. Debentures, including debenture stock, loan stock, bonds, certificates of deposit and other instrument creating or acknowledging indebtedness, not being instruments falling within paragraph 3 below* i.e. debt securities issued by a government, local authority or public authority.

Note. This paragraph shall not be construed as applying:

(a) to any instrument acknowledging or creating indebtedness for, or for money borrowed to defray, the consideration payable under a contract for the supply of goods or services;

---

* N.B. paragraph 3 still applies for this purpose

(b) to a cheque or other bill of exchange, a banker's draft or a letter of credit; or

(c) to a banknote, a statement showing a balance in a current, deposit or savings account or (by reason of any financial obligation contained in it) to a lease or other disposition of property, a heritable security or an insurance policy.

3. [omitted]

Instruments entitling to shares or securities

4. Warrants or other instruments entitling the holder to subscribe for investments falling within paragraph 1 or 2 above.

Notes.

(1) It is immaterial whether the investments are for the time being in existence or identifiable.

(2) An investment falling within this paragraph shall not be regarded as falling with paragraphs 7, 8 or 9 below.

(3) This paragraph applies only to instruments issued by the person issuing the investment to be subscribed for.

Certificates or other instruments which confer:

(a) property rights in respect of any investment falling within paragraphs 1, 2, 3 or 4 above.

(b) any right to acquire, dispose of, underwrite or convert such an investment, being a right to which the holder would be entitled if he held any such investment to which the certificate or instrument relates; or

(c) a contractual right (other than an option) to acquire any such investment otherwise than by subscription.

<u>Note</u>. This paragraph does not apply to any instrument which confers rights in respect of two or more investments issued by different persons.

Appendix 3

<table>
<tr><th>Offers on admission to dealings on an ARIE</th><th>Primary Offers</th><th>Secondary Offers</th></tr>
<tr><td colspan="3">(a) advertisement such that no agreement can be entered into until a prospectus delivered;
(b) offer conditional on admission to listing under Part IV;
(c) other securities issued by same issuer dealt in on an ARIE and ARIE certifies that sufficient information available to investors;
(d) advertisement falls within section 58(2);
(e) order made by the Secretary of State in cases where foreign law provides equivalent protection (section 161(4)).</td></tr>
<tr><td></td><td colspan="2">regulations exempting advertisements:
(a) having private character;
(b) dealing with investments only incidentally;
(c) issued to persons sufficiently expert to understand any risks;
(d) relating to investments of a kind normally bought or dealt in by persons sufficiently expert to understand any risks; or
(e) other classes.</td></tr>
<tr><td>(a) where a prospectus filed in the previous 12 months and ARIE certifies that sufficient information available to investors;
or
(b) where the securities listed in accordance with Part IV in the previous 12 months and ARIE gives a similar certificate</td><td></td><td>Prospectus filed in the past six months in respect of a primary or secondary offer of those securities.</td></tr>
</table>

Michael Robinson

I have only four small comments and they all involve what might happen in the future pursuant to Ralph's extremely good paper.

The first one is the fascinating prospect of whether the driftiest of the prospectuses in the United Kingdom will end up drafting documents full of boring disclaimers and warnings like is done in North America because the regulators all read the things and require this sort of disclaimer language to go in, or whether because of the brilliant idea of not allowing the SIB or anyone else to screen the document and pre-clear it we will let the beauty of Her Majesty's language, as practised in the United Kingdom where it is practised best, to triumph and we will get a genuinely readable document. That is a really interesting prospect to me. I would think that when one looks at some of the Draconian remedies in your bifurcated system where it is self-regulation (except that if you do it wrong you go directly to jail), I think that we may start finding that your draftsmen start using all of this sort of disclaimer and weasel words and we may end up with a US, Canadian (North American) type document which, as we all know, nobody but an expert can read and few even do.

Point two, the private placement list to be developed by the DTI. I would commend those who may speak for the DTI to think in terms of setting a specific list rather than using a whole bunch of general categories. This I think was one of the better things which we did in Canada as opposed to the United States where they have one of these floating definitions of what is private. We have a specific list of transactions done with certain sophisticated people over a certain size in certain types of securities that are exempt. You don't have to have the prospectus and people know what they are doing. It also helps the lawyers because we give legal opinions that the transaction falls within an exception for which we charge, of course, modest fees.

Point three, I was interested in what is going to happen in your remedy area because I noted that there doesn't seem to be a rescission right clearly put in the statute. It's a right to compensation and I think that's an oversight because for many investors (the widow and orphan) need simple rescission rather than some action for damages where you have to prove causation and the specificity of the damages. Now perhaps the rescission right continues to exist in common law and Ralph can perhaps correct me here But I didn't see it in his paper as a statutory right.

I am also interested in the exemptions from liability and I wonder if we are going to end up with a duediligence type of function in the United Kingdom that is practised in Canada where the underwriters all run around and count the bricks and kick the tyres and examine all the documents and add horrendously to the fees of the underwriters' lawyers. I gather the UK way is much more sensible, one sits down in a room and drafts a document and talks to the company people and believes what they say, at least after some limited cross-examination, versus the American way which exists because there is a defence of dueduligence, and the dueness of the diligence is carried to quite extraordinary lengths.

The last comment is to wonder if it would be useful in the United Kingdom to consider some sort of system like that in North America. We call it by the wonderful acronym - acronyms are very popular today - the POP system, pre-offering prospectus qualification system, where we have a standard document that is on file for a sophisticated issuer, filed annually and updated from time to time and not distributed to the purchasers unless they ask for it, which contains all the core things like the famous US Form S.1. The short-term prospectus for these larger, more sophisticated issuers can be prepared very quickly and promptly and does not need all the voluminous disclosure that is in a normal prospectus.

Dr. Hans Rudolf Steiner

1. Issuance of Shares and Stock

(1) Formation of a New Company

If the shares of a newly formed company are offered to the public Article 631 of the Swiss Code of Obligations (CO) applies. This Article reads as follows:

"In the event that shares are offered for public subscription, a prospectus (Art. 651) signed by all founders shall be made.

This prospectus shall set forth: 1. Prospectus

1. The clauses in the Articles of Incorporation required by law to be included (Art. 626) as well as the clauses which must appear in the Articles of Incorporation in order to be valid (Arts. 627, 628);
2. Contributions in kind, acquisition of assets immediately after incorporation and benefits of founders, if any (Art. 628);
3. The essential elements of the report of the founders (Art. 630);
4. The date until which a subscription is binding;
5. The places where subscriptions may be made;
6. The issue price of shares (Arts. 624, 622);
7. The amount to be paid in on shares prior to the incorporation meeting of the subscribers (Art. 633);
8. The places where payments on shares may be effected.

A special prospectus may be dispensed with if the subscription certificates contain the names of all founders and the information prescribed in this Article (Art. 632)".

Article 631 refers to certain additional Articles of the CO, the most important of which are:

Article 626 CO:

"The Articles of Incorporation shall contain clauses concerning the following matters:

1. The company name (Arts. 950, 951) and the address of the registered office of the Company (Swiss Civil Code Art. 56);
2. The object and the purpose of the enterprise;
3. The amount of the capital stock and the par value (Art. 622) of individual shares, the type of shares (Art. 622) and, as appropriate, the number (Art. 622, para. 2) of registered and bearer shares;
4. The procedure for calling a General Meeting of Stockholders and the voting rights of the stockholders;
5. The bodies which are to manage (Art. 707 et seq.) and to audit (Art. 727 et seq.) the Company and the manner in which the Company is to be represented (Art. 717 et seq.);
6. The number of qualifying shares to be deposited by each member of the Board of Directors (Arts. 709, 710);
7. The manner in which the Company publishes its official notices".

and Article 627 CO:

Clauses regulating the following matters are only valid if they appear in the Article of Incorporation.

"1. Deviations from the normal legal provisions concerning changes of the Articles of Incorporation, particularly with respect to expansion or restriction of the objects of the Company, increases or reductions in the capital stock and changes of the normal legal provisions concerning a merger (Art. 647-658, 732-734, 748-750);
2. Clauses concerning the sharing of the Board of Directors in the net profits of the Company (Art 677);
3. Payment of interest out of capital stock during construction periods (Art. 676);
4. Limitation of the duration of the Company;
5. Fixing of the amount to be paid-in on shares if higher than the legal minimum (Art. 633);
6. Rules concerning penalties in case the subscribed capital is not paid-in within the stated time (Arts. 681, 682);
7. The possibility to convert registered shares into bearer shares and vice-versa (Art. 622);
8. The prohibition of, or restrictions on the transfer of registered shares (Arts. 684-688);
9. Clauses concerning the issue of preferred shares (Arts. 654-656), profit sharing certificates (Arts. 657, 658), and founders shares (Art. 628);
10. Restrictions on voting rights (Arts. 692, para. 3, 691), and the rights of a stockholder to appoint a proxy (Arts. 689 - 691), as well as restrictions on the issue of voting shares (Art. 693);

11. Clauses whereby the General Meeting of Stockholders may pass certain resolutions only with a qualified majority in addition to the cases provided for by law;
12. The power of the Board of Directors to delegate its authority to individual members of the Board or to third persons (Arts. 717 et seq.);
13. Clauses concerning the organisation, rights and duties of the auditors (Art. 727 et seq.), if such rules exceed the requirements established by law".

and Article 628 CO:

"If a stockholder does not pay cash for his shares, the Article of Incorporation (Art. 636) must state the identify of the assets contributed, their value, and the amount credited by the Company for such assets to the stockholders, as well as the name of the person making the contribution in kind and the number of shares issued to such person in exchange for such assets.

If the Company is to acquire assets from stockholders or third persons immediately after incorporation, the Articles of Incorporation (Art. 636) shall indicate the assets to be acquired, the name of the transferor and the consideration to be paid by the Company.

If, upon incorporation, particular benefits are granted to the founders or other persons, the Articles of Incorporation (Arts. 627, sub-para. 9, 636) shall list the names of such persons and the type of benefits as well as their value".

and Article 630 CO:

"If part or all of the capital stock consists of contributions in kind, or if the Company is to acquire assets immediately after incorporation, or if special benefits are to be granted to founders or other persons (Arts. 628, 631, para. 2, sub-para. 2, 636), the founders shall issue a detailed written report.

The report shall contain detailed information on the following facts where applicable:

1. The identify and conditions of the assets to be contributed or acquired and the basis of their valuation;
2. The number of shares to be issued in exchange or any other consideration to be given by the Company.
3. The reasons for creating benefits for founders or third persons and how the basis for valuation was determined.

The original of the report of the founders or a certified copy thereof shall be open for inspection at each place (Art. 631, para. 2, sub-para. 5) where subscriptions are taken.

(2) Increase of Share Capital

In case of an existing company increasing its share capital by issuing new shares to the public Article 651 CO applies, which reads as follows:

Art. 651. Any offer of shares to the public must be made by means of a prospectus by which the public is invited to subscribe which shall be signed by a duly authorised representative of the Company in the name of the Board of Directors".

The prospectus must contain the following information (Art. 631 CO):

1. Date of registration in the Commercial Register;
2. Name and registered office of the Company;
3. Previous amount and composition of the capital stock, indicating per value of shares, kind and classes of shares and preferential rights, if any:
4. Profit sharing certificates, if any, and their rights;
5. Listing of the Board of Directors and auditors;
6. Latest balance sheet and profit and loss statement together with the auditors' report;
7. Dividends paid during the past five years or, if the Company has existed less than five years, since the foundation of the Company;
8. Any debentures issued by the Company;
9. The resolution authorising the new issue of shares including total amount, par value, and issue price, as well as number and type of the new shares;
10. Contributions in kind, acquisition of assets, and preferential rights;
11. Date from which the new shares rank for dividend purposes and restrictions of the right to receive dividends and preferential rights, if any;
12. Date until which the subscription is binding.

A special prospectus may be dispensed with (Art. 631) if the above information is contained in the subscription form.

(3) Application of Articles 631 and 651 CO

The Swiss Code of Obligations does not require any prospectus for a public offering of shares of stock of foreign companies (neither primary nor secondary). According to the opinion of the most important legal scholars no prospectus is required either in case of a secondary offering of shares of stock of a Swiss Company. However, in practice hardly any secondary offering takes place without a prospectus, and there is a real risk that the courts might apply the prospectus requirement to secondary offerings by analogy.

2. Issuance of Bonds

With regard to the issuance of bonds (and similar debt securities issued in series) Article 1156 CO requires a prospectus whether or not the issuer is a Swiss Company.

Article 1156 CO reads as follows:

"Bonds may only be submitted for a public subscription or introduced on the stock exchange based upon a prospectus.

The provisions concerning the prospectus for the issue of new shares (Arts. 651, 752) are to be applied by analogy. Moreover, the prospectus must contain the detailed information concerning the loan, especially the interest terms, terms of repayment, special security provided for the bonds, and the representation (Arts. 1158-1162), of any, of the bond creditors.

If bonds are issued without a prospectus complying with these provisions, or if the prospectus contains incorrect information or information not in accordance with the legal requirements, the persons who intentionally or negligently took part, are liable (Arts. 752, 759) jointly and severally for damages".

With regard to Notes in denominations of SFr. 50,000, and more to be placed by the underwriting banks with their own customers, the Swiss banks adopted a convention which contains some additional requirements. Thus the prospectus has to indicate, among other things, the development of the borrower's business since the end of the last fiscal year if more than six months have elapsed, and to inform about the listing of the borrower's stock in his home country and high/low stock prices quoted over the last three years, if the Notes are equity related, and to indicate the rating of the borrower.

3. Prospectus Requirement for Listing at a Swiss Stock Exchange

The new uniform listing regulations applying to listings on all Swiss stock exchanges require a listing prospectus for all types of securities to be listed. Such prospectus must comply with paragraph 8 of the regulations which goes beyond the requirements of Articles 631, 651 and 1156 CO and reads as follows:

Para. 8

"8.1 The listing prospectus shall enable investors to assess the quality of the security proposed for listing. The investors must be able to obtain the prospectus free of charge, either in the German, French, Italian or English language at least from the Stock Exchange member filing the application.

8.2 The prospectus shall contain the following data and information concerning the Issuer:

(a) Details of the legal personality of the issuing company (name, registered office, duration, date of entry in the Commercial Register or registration with an equivalent foreign authority), description of its activities and information where securities of the issuer embodying equity participation rights are listed (such as convertible bond issues, warrant issues), a record of the stock market development of these equity rights during the last five years must be stated.

(b) The presentation of the capital resources of the issuer (amount and composition of the capital, reserves, other equity funds, etc.) with details regarding preferential rights, dividend-right certificates and similar entitlements.

(c) The voting rules.

(d) The composition of the Supervisory Authorities the Management and the Auditors.

(e) The dividends and similar benefits paid during the last five years (or since the company was founded).

(f) Summary details regarding the public bond issues placed by the issuer (currency, amount, date of maturity), stating also the collateral security and privileges to the extent these are not mentioned under (b).

(g) The fiscal year and balance sheet accounting principles applied by the issuer.

(h) The most recent audited - and, if published, consolidated - balance sheet and income statement (including contingent liabilities) and the report of the Auditors.

(i) Those subsidiary and group companies whose shareholders' equity make up at least 5% of the assets of the issuer or 100 million Swiss francs, stating the shareholder and equity conditions and the capital resources of these companies.

(k) In the event that more than six months have passed since the last audited annual closing, the most recently published quarterly or semi-annual closing statement or, if not available, a report on the current fiscal year.

In the case of entities organised under public law, at least the assets, the income and the expenditures, as well as any budget figures approved by the competent authorities, shall be stated. Complete data must be furnished in the case of exceptions within the meaning of section 2.5; these may be shortened for the issuer.

8.3 The admission prospectus shall contain the following information on the security:

(a) The legal basis for the placement of the securities and, in the case of foreign issuers, the applicable law and the place of jurisdiction.

(b) Description of the security: security number, legal structure of the security and the ancillary rights, total principal amount and par values, warrants, coupons, etc.; in the case of securities made out to name (registered securities), information concerning restrictions on transfers. Should such restrictions be material, the series and the numbers shall also be listed.

(c) In the case of shares (equities) and similar securities a summary description of the voting rights and possible obligations to pay the unpaid-for portion of the par value; the loan terms and conditions for bonds and similar securities shall be listed in full (including interest calculations, possible conversion rights, warrant rights etc.).

(d) The designation of the paying agent(s) in Zurich.

(e) The description of the kind and legal nature of collateral security, if any.

(f) The obligation to publish in a newspaper regularly appearing in Zurich in good time all notifications arising from the security.

(g) Mentioning of the listing application and the name of other stock exchanges on which the security is already listed and where listing will be applied for".

The listing regulations do not require the prospectus to be published in any newspapers but only to be available at the counters of the banks accepting subscriptions. Instead an abbreviated version, the so-called "listing advertisement" must be published. Because the listing prospectus can be in German, French, Italian or English it may be possible to use a prospectus prepared for a foreign listing and add a "wrap-up" containing only those items referring specifically to the Swiss listing and those required by the Swiss regulation but not contained in the main prospectus.

4. Liability

"If, on the occasion of the formation of a Company, or of the issuance of shares or bonds, there have been made or divulged statements in a prospectus (Arts. 631, 651), or in circulars, or similar notifications, which are incorrect or do not comply with the legal requirements, anyone who has co-operated intentionally or negligently in this connection will be liable to the individual stockholders or bondholders for damage caused thereby".

With regard to bonds the third paragraph of Article 1156 quoted above applies also.

Article 759 CO reads as follows:

"If several persons are responsible for the same damages, they shall be jointly and severally liable.

The recourse among several participants will be decided by the judge according to the degree of fault of the individual".

A liability can be invoked by persons who suffered a damage because the prospectus did not comply with the legal requirements, if they can show that the defendant caused the damage intentionally or negligently. The available defences are similar to those in English Law. The most important ones are that the defendant could not know of the misstatement or omission, or that plaintiff knew of it. A defendant paying the full amount of damages due to the joint and several liability will have recourse to his co-defendants in accordance with the relative responsibility for the damage in question. Although the number of cases involving the liability of corporate directors and auditors has increased dramatically over the last few years and the courts have adopted a rather strict line in favour of plaintiffs, prospectus liability cases are extremely rare.

The process of securitisation and the access of second and third rate borrowers to the capital market may, however, change this in the near future.

Conclusion

In comparison Swiss prospectus rules are still rather simple. Combined with liberal accounting standards Switzerland provides an attractive legal framework for new issues and stock exchange listings. Over-regulations of the London market by the SRO's and further reduction of Swiss stamp duties may improve the competitive position of the Swiss market and affect London's position in the Eurobond market.

Andre Newburg

I think that from the US perspective in the Eurobond market that generally speaking we are more concerned with protecting against civil liabilities and there are more securities laws than any particular compliance problem. I think that generally speaking US issuers have not countered great difficulties in meeting the prospectus requirements of foreign exchanges including the London Stock Exchange and I would not expect that the new prospectus requirements would create any difficulties for listed issuers. What interests me is whether FSA deals at all with civil liabilities in connection with the offer of sale of securities unrelated to where there is no prospectus delivered, or if that is left up to common law.

Simon macLachlan

I think the answer is that it is left to common law except that in so far as the offer or sale contravenes the rules of the SRO or the SIB then there might be a liability under section 62.

Andre Newburg

I see, even where there is no prospectus delivered.

Simon macLachlan

It could be, not necessarily, it depends what happens.

CONFLICTS AND CHINESE WALLS

John Robertson

As you will have learnt, the two main recent happenings have been first of all Big Bang, which came about primarily as a result of the vastly increased international competition (and it was triggered by the agreement between the Government and the Stock Exchange in July 1983 to move to negotiated commissions by not later than December 1986) and the second main happening is the impending introduction of the Financial Services Act. This is the culmination of several years work, starting off with Professor Gowers' report. Now we are faced with this very complex legislation which, according to the latest timetable, is due to come into place in April 1988.

The three years or so between the 1983 agreement and Big Bang in October 1986 sounds a long time in a way but it was an incredibly short time for all the huge and radical changes that were due to come about. No sensible business man in his right mind would have planned to pack so many major changes into such a short space of time. We got there and we are still reasonably alive and I think possibly reasonably honest too! The fact that these two major happenings, Big Bang and the Financial Services Act, are roughly coinciding, a year and a half apart, is, in my view, a happy coincidence. Even though the process was started off as a result of failures by a number of licensed dealers it is very appropriate that, because of the new dual capacity world, we have got a new regulatory framework to ensure that everyone sticks to the straight and narrow.

Let's make no mistake about it, the new framework is going to be incredibly complicated. It does fall short of a full SEC system and is often described as a practitioner based statutory framework. In other words, there is a major element of practitioner input. One of the main difficulties is being caused by section 62 of the Act. This essentially says that anyone who suffers a loss may sue a member of an SRO for being in breach of that SRO's rules. This caused quite a heated discussion some months ago among those of us who are practitioners on one particular SRO, the TSA, who felt quite strongly that the principal purpose of a rule book should be to tell those members of an association what they could and couldn't do and that meant that they had to be able to understand it. Because of section 62, our lawyers advised us very strongly that it was absolutely paramount that those rules of the TSA had to be legally watertight, for they would undoubtedly be tested in a court of law. So here we are with a very complicated set of rules that, even for those of us who are involved with the thing quite a lot, are difficult to interpret. I can't tell you how difficult it is going to be for our players at the sharp end of the business. You could say that this regulatory act and all the framework is a lawyer's paradise but I should probably not say that in this company!

I believe that, notwithstanding all the rules and regulations, the handling of conflicts of interest is basically a question of common sense. We are very much on a learning curve because the extra number of conflicts that we are faced with, largely with market-making coming in under the same roof with distribution and research, is quite a new thing for us. I believe also that the disciplines of the market place will rule. In other words, you could say that we are now in a period of enlightened self-interest where if we do the dirty on a client once and we get caught, we might just about get away with it and that client would go on giving us business. But do it a second time and get caught again, then we are out and deservedly so. Let us now look at the role of compliance in this whole area of conflicts.

At a time of great business change and competitive pressures we are in the United Kingdom also to experience this new regulatory system, a regime which although based on practitioner involvement will be considerably more formalised and may in the formative early period have to face its greatest challenge by proving itself sufficiently flexible. As the draft rules emerge it is clear that the regulators will expect to see a compliance function within firms. The larger the firm the more dedicated the compliance resources must be, while in smaller firms it might be a part time involvement with the individuals concerned. This regulatory desire for compliance units serves to underline the fact that they are perceived as a further layer of the regulatory structure. However, many larger houses in the City of London appointed compliance offers and established divisions to cover compliance some year to eighteen months ago, although this was not as a direct response to the prospects of having to cope with myriad rules. The main reason that compliance divisions were perceived as necessary was so as to prove to clients that the organisation would be able to handle properly the numerous additional conflicts of interest. The introduction of dual capacity on the Stock Exchange was perhaps the most severe jolt to the system with the management of a firms' own assets in addition to providing services to and dealing for clients and looking after their assets.

That is not to say that dual capacity was an entirely new experience but it was largely a total change for Stock Exchange member firms. While there were considerably more conflicts arising from companies outside the Stock Exchange being allowed by the authorities to purchase Stock Exchange firms it should be noted that there remain three basic categories. One, the interest of one client versus that of another, two, the interest of the house versus that of the client and three, the interest of staff versus those of the client and of the house. Additional conflicts of interest are but variations on these three themes.

Irrespective of the fact that the rules of the regulatory authorities will be designed to protect the interest of clients it will be clear that the law of agency must also apply to client relationships. Therefore, those compliance divisions first into the field have been involved in examining fiduciary obligations and drawing up client agreements which effectively codify the protection that a client should automatically enjoy under common law in the United Kingdom, at the same time making due disclosure of conflicts so that dual capacity and agency obligations can coexist. Greater disclosure is one of the key factors of the new regime.

The earlier reference to managing conflicts should be noted, because in the deregulated financial markets, which a number of financial centres have introduced or are about so to do, the conflicts can generally not be avoided. Indeed deregulation invariably introduces conflicts. There is increasing reference to that element of corporate architecture known as Chinese Walls. These are devices for helping to separate centres of knowledge in a multi-faceted business - the duty of confidentially which is owed to clients. Chinese Walls are typified in various ways by corporate structure, e.g. conflicting business conducted in separately incorporated units, by physical separation and by culture. Chinese Walls, however, are of finite height. Once confidential information has been made public it is essential that the procedures prevent influence from being applied. For example, prior to an announcement of a take-over bid, information is price sensitive and should not be divulged by those in possession of it. However, once an announcement is made it is still necessary to ensure that other areas of the firm are not persuaded to take supporting action or perhaps feel themselves to be duty bound to support the corporate finance client. This emphasis on conflicts of interest and the duty owed to clients should be fully recognised because the compliance division is one of the main sources of protection. Perhaps the other main protection is competition because a tarnished reputation is a quick way to lose custom. Conflicts of interest and their resolution are perhaps the most important aspects of the compliance divisions work. It stems from the judgment necessary to resolve an imbalance of interest in conflicting situations through to surveillance. The division must always be prepared to be the arbitrator of the best practice no matter how unpopular that decision. The title of compliance officer is arguably a misnomer for the main responsibility of compliance is borne by the line management of the business divisions of an investment firm whether it is dealing with clients or running a book. There is nothing new in that concept because it is the proper role of management to bear responsibility for ensuring that business is undertaken not only in an efficient manner and to meet the targets laid down, but also within the requirements of legislation and any rules and regulations that apply to the firm. If the operating divisions fail to have an instinct for what is acceptable practice or that which is beyond the rules or they recklessly breach the rules the compliance division can be no more than a first aid post which has to patch up relations with an injured client and just as seriously has to do its best to treat the bruised reputation of the firm. It cannot be emphasised strongly enough that it is the departments that deal with the clients who are the guardians of best practice whilst it is the compliance division that will stand guard over them and the client's interest.

I have tried to draw a distinction between those conflicts of interest under the old regime and under the new. Single capacity before Big Bang, was where salesmen, analysts and market-makers worked for different firms, with no common ownership and practically no conflict of interest. This very rigid separation of capacity between the principal and agent was perhaps quite an elegant solution to removing one particular conflict. But now that rigid separation is gone we have to learn how to handle it.

On investment management there was a very uneven playing field in that investment management and broking firms only had access to their own house research whereas the investment management arm of the merchants banks, who accounted for the vast majority of asset management, had access to all brokers' research. In addition, the charging structure was different in that the broker was remunerated out of his commission every time he dealt whereas the merchant bank would get maybe a modest share of the broker's commission but also charged an annual management fee.

Corporate finance: well there is nothing much really new there between the old and new regime. As I said earlier, it is confined to merchant banks and brokers and these Chinese Walls existed and I don't think it is being too complacent to say that in the main they always worked pretty well. I believe that Chinese Walls are referred to as "fire walls" by Alan Greenspan. A few years ago, when we first start thinking about Chinese Walls, they were referred to as "green baize doors". I remember asking the head of the investment management arm of a prestigious merchant bank whether he was in a separate building to his opposite number in the corporate finance side or different floors or whatever, and he said: "you must be joking, I share a desk with him and we know how to manage the conflicts". So how times have changed!

Under the new regime, we have investment banking conglomerates offering merchant banking, broking, research and market-making all under the same roof and this is where most of the difficulties arise.

The new Chinese Walls between broking and market-making: two main points here - one is the position of the market-makers book position and whether that is available to the salesman and the analyst. In our house, and I think in most houses, it is not widely known because that enables the salesman better to advise his client without any particular axe to grind knowing what the house's position is. Also, a very interesting area is that of front running: whether research material is released to salesmen and market-makers ahead of the public impact or not. As I understand it, in the United States front running listed securities is forbidden whereas in OTC stocks it's permitted. In the United Kingdom we are aiming to tackle this problem in a different way in that, provided you notify your client in the client agreement letter that you might possibly at times front-run, you can do it. The SIB and TSA rules both have something to say on this, you can do it to the extent that it is necessary to anticipate order flow from clients and provided you don't materially disturb the price in the market. Both of those two things are, as you can imagine, very difficult to actually forecast because who knows what the order flow is going to be. There may be a nil response to your research recommendation. So it would be very difficult and subjective to follow that rule but at least SIB and TSA are doing their best to try and enable it to happen provided people behave responsibly and sensibly.

Investment management is very firmly behind Chinese Walls, different buildings in most cases and the playing field has been levelled in that they do now have access to research from all broking houses that they care to go to.

Corporate finance: not much has altered here really. Very high and impenetrable Chinese Walls and we have to be very careful when we bring research analysts or salesmen across that wall. This sometimes happens because they have a particular contact with a person in a corporate client, which is the cause of some quite major difficulties which we have had. Also in that department we, and I think most houses, have a prior permission regime for personal account dealings and generally compliance is monitoring it as an area of sensitivity.

On the banking side, commercial banking should be entirely separate from the investment division. Information about clients should remain totally discrete but, having said that, there is clearly scope for a mutual encouragement of business by bringing in clients to various parts of the business. We in this country, largely for historical reasons, have no such thing as a Glass Steagall Act (USA) or

Article 65 (Japan). Certainly if, in the fullness of time, it is found that commercial banking and investment banking cannot work side by side then undoubtedly we will have legislation to separate the two. When I tell you that the Glass Steagall Act came into effect in 1934 and 1934 is the year in which I was born, you will realise that the Glass Steagall Act has got a bit rusty. The fact that we are free from any such legislation does mean, in my view, that it should help to make London a major centre of the global market, free from any excessive restrictions providing always that we handle conflicts of interest properly.

Joni Nelson

I would like to split my comments into two parts. The first part is perhaps to summarise the arguments for the Glass Steagall idea of separation. Glass Steagall was a response, as has been said, to the perceived need for a separation between commercial banking and investment banking activities but similar arguments could be made for a separation between dealing and broking in securities, which is the area upon which our discussions have been focused.

After I have described the arguments which can be made for the Glass Steagall separation, I will explain the political ramifications, why things are where they are in the United States today and the impact of the new banking act enacted this summer.

Glass Steagall came into being after the Great Depression following the collapse of the securities market in 1929 and the ensuing collapse of a vast number of banks. Congress concluded first, that there was a connection, that there had been a exacerbation of the market collapse because the banks had been underwriting and investing in the securities. On the other hand, the separation enacted by Congress may have produced merely the illusion of protection for the banking system. I doubt if the repercussions today would be any less if for instance, a firm like Drexel

Burnham (which is itself highly leveraged) were to go under. Banks have lent extensively not only in connection with the buy-outs arranged by the investment banks, but also to the investment banks themselves, secured in many cases by the junk bonds which these institutions have underwritten.

Secondly, Congress felt that there was a temptation for lenders to make soft loans to shore up shaky investment banking clients. (On the other hand, in the light of current developments in the United States in the field of creditor's liability a bank would today make such loans at its peril. So this is perhaps not as strong a temptation as it was when Congress was looking at the situation).

The third argument was that investment advice to the bank's clients would be biased in favour of the securities of companies which the bank had underwritten or in which it had made an investment. The same argument would seem to apply equally to investment advice concerning securities of borrowers, or for that matter, investment advice by investment banking firms, both of which Congress was content to regulate rather than prohibit.

Fourth, it was feared that banks would encourage shaky borrowers to underwrite issues of securities in order to facilitate the payment of loans to the commercial banking side of the institution, and at the same time the bank would take another group of fees at the front end of the transaction.

The fifth argument was the potential for stuffing unsold securities into the trust department of the bank. And sixth was the paradox in sharing information about a client among various arms of the financial institution. The sharing of information is, I might add, a very real problem today because under Glass Steagall US commercial banks are allowed to (and do) maintain investment banks in foreign countries. If, for instance, the commercial banking side of the institution has put a borrower on some sort of watch list at the same time as the investment banking side is about to underwrite a Eurocommercial paper facility, the conflicts of interest, disclosure requirements and shared information problems are serious.

These arguments raised in Congress have considerable merit. On the other hand the real reason that Glass Steagall has not been amended has little to do with the merits. If the decision had been based upon the merits of the argument, the legislation would not be limited to a one-way street. If the conflicts and dangers in permitting the same entity to carry on both commercial and investment banking are too intense to be merely regulated by rules for disclosure and Chinese Walls, then not only should Citibank be prohibited from owning Goldman Sachs, but also Merrill Lynch should not be permitted to own banks (which it does). There is no intellectual justification for allowing Bankers Trust to underwrite commercial paper issues in foreign markets if it is too great a threat to the stability of the banking system for it to do so in the United States.

The real reason that Glass Steagall survives albeit as a one-way street within water's edge, is due to the political nature of the statute, and the competitive interests of the constituencies which are pushing for change. For the most part, the large banks have lobbied for repeal of Glass Steagall, but the smaller local banks regard it as protection for them against potential competition from the mega-banks. Thus the banking industry has been divided on this issue. Second, the securities and investment banking industries do speak with one voice and they are lobbying furiously against repeal because they do not want any further competition. And third, separate committees in Congress oversee each of these activities and the committee chairmen do not want to lose their power structure.

As a result, despite the efforts to get Glass Steagall revoked, what emerged this summer is something called the Competitive Equality Banking Act of 1987. Because Congress deals in euphemisms (e.g., the Bank Secrecy Act took away all bank secrecy and the Tax Reduction Act raised taxes), the Competitive Equality Act did not create equality between banks and the investment banks. Instead we have a standstill on the expansion of banking activities until 1st March, 1988, with respect to both the non-bank banks, as they are known (i.e. those which do not both accept deposits and make commercial loans), as well as the implementation of the approvals already granted by the Federal Reserve Board to banking institutions e.g. to underwrite and deal in mortgage-backed securities and municipal bonds and to place commercial paper through a subsidiary. Banks may not until 1st March, 1988, carry on any activity in which they were not engaged on 5th March, 1987. There is a great deal of lobbying on this issue, but many people think that the standstill may be extended by Congress.

Underlying this problem is the fact that Glass Steagall was written at a time when Merrill Lynch had not thought about going into the banking business, Sears Roebuck had not thought about entering investment banking, and General Motors had not thought about financing its own cars let alone home mortgages. The United States should tidy up its legislation in light of the realities of today's international financial services industry.

There are still valid arguments to be made for the separation of commercial banking from investment banking functions. If we have many more Boesky-like scandals, or the Stock Market tumbles, the tide for repealing Glass Steagall may come to a halt and we may end up with more rather than less restrictions in the United States. So at a time when England, France, Germany and Canada are washing away all barriers and separations and relying on Chinese Walls, there is a chance that the United States could be erecting Berlin Walls between all these functions within the financial services industry.

<u>Simon macLachlan</u>

There is one point I'd like to get an answer to is. We have heard talk of the 'watch list' and the 'stop list' as I understand the UK rules that doesn't as such exist or does it?

<u>John Robertson</u>

I don't think there any rules as such that I am aware of but I think the practice amongst different houses does differ. In our own organisation, for example, we don't operate any restrictions because we feel that if somebody wants to do a personal account deal and they are told they can't because its on some particular list, then that would actually give the game away to people that there is something going on, but there are a lot of houses who do operate this kind of system.

<u>Joni Nelson</u>

We have, as you know, a restrictive list, the theory being that by the time a security is on a restrictive list, the game has probably been given away to all sorts of institutions which are trading many more shares than Aunt Minnie. Aunt Minnie is probably the only person who doesn't know what's going on, so it is better to restrict the firm which is putting together the deal from broking at that point.

<u>Simon macLachlan</u>

But it is clear, is it not, that there is no liability to the client who suffers because his normal broking house is not able to deal?

Joni Nelson

Well, the customer could go to another broking house, certainly the argument is there that putting someone on the restrictive list lets you know that something is up but its a lesser evil.

Noboru Nakagawa

1. Banks and Securities Companies

The well-quoted provisions of Article 65 of the Securities and Exchange Law of Japan (SEL) state that banks, trusts banks, insurance companies and other designated financial institutions are prohibited from conducting securities business except in limited circumstances. From the other end, Article 43 of SEL provides that securities companies may not conduct any business other than securities business, unless previously approved by the Minister of Finance in certain limited circumstances. The Banking Law of Japan, on the other hand, provides that banks may conduct only banking business and certain other designated or related businesses.

This is effectively a reflection of the American legislation concerning the separation of banking and securities business and has been strictly enforced for a number of years until recently. However, due to the trend of deregularisation and liberalisations, the barrier between the business of banks and securities companies is being gradually eroded. A typical example is the fact that now banks are permitted to transact business in government bonds to a limited extent. Both banks and securities companies will be soon allowed to deal in commercial papers issued in Japan by Japanese companies.

There are a number of branches in Japan of foreign securities companies which are fully owned by foreign securities companies or merchant banks. Japanese law and the Ministry of Finance did not, for a long time, allow foreign securities companies' branches to be established in Japan if they were owned or controlled by foreign banks. However, this policy was changed a few years ago and now it is the policy of the Ministry of Finance that the foreign banks can own up to 50% of a foreign securities company which establishes a securities branch in Japan and obtain Japanese security licences, on condition that the remaining 50% of the shares is owned by a totally unrelated company or companies, such as industrial or commercial companies, and that the directors of the head office of the securities company are not employees of, or otherwise closely associated with foreign banks.

In respect of Japanese securities companies, four of the largest Japanese securities companies are generally considered to be effectively independent from any Japanese banks. A number of less larger but still well-established securities companies are independent from banks, but some of the medium-sized securities companies have a close connection with banks. Due to Article 11 of the Japanese Anti-monopoly Law, banks (and securities companies) may not own more than 5% of shares in another company. But, using a carefully designed shareholding structure, banks can have more or less some close relationship with "their own" securities companies.

In any event, securities companies, whether Japanese or foreign, are separate legal entities from banks and under the present Japanese legislation they are competing with each other for the purpose of providing finance to industrial and commercial companies. Therefore the problem of conflict of interest is less acute in Japan.

2. Securities Companies

Within a securities company itself, pursuant to the presently effective provisions of SEL, licences are divided broadly into four categories, namely underwriting licence, broking licence, dealing licence and offering licence. However, SEL allows that any securities company can have one or more of these four licences. There can be, therefore, a certain degree of conflict of interest within a securities company between the broking and dealing departments.

SEL contains certain protection of investors from the combination of dealing and broking activities of securities companies. Article 65 of SEL provides that a securities company when receiving an order from a customer, must clearly specify to the customer as to whether the securities company will act as a dealer and sell or buy securities between itself and its customer or simply act as a broker in the market. Also, Article 47 of SEL provides that no securities company may act at the same time as principal and broker or agent of a counterparty in connection with the same sale or buying transaction of securities. The Tokyo Stock Exchange and other stock exchanges prescribe in their rules a similar restriction on dealing and broking for the purpose of prevention of conflict of interest. The Ministry of Finance issues administrative guidances to securities companies recommending them not to conduct excessive dealings.

3. Securities Investment Advisory Services

A new law introduced in 1986 concerning regulation on securities investment advisory services contains a set of rules on advisory services on securities investment. The service had not been regulated before the law came into effect in November, 1986. Securities companies and banks are not permitted to conduct investment advisory services, because, as mentioned above, banks and securities companies are prohibited from conducting any business other than banking and securities businesses, respectively, unless specifically authorised by express provisions of laws or by approvals of the Ministry of Finance. This does not prevent the banks and securities companies from holding shares in investment advisory service companies. This means that again investment advisory service companies are separate legal entities and, as such, there can be no conflict of interest if we look only within such companies.

In respect of their relationship with other institutions, there are certain provisions in the said law concerning regulation of investment advisory services. Article 18 of the law provides that an investment advisor may not sell, or buy, or otherwise deal in securities with its own clients in relation to its advisory services. An investment advisor may not receive from its clients cash or securities nor procure the clients' money or securities to be deposited with companies related to the advisor, such as its principal shareholders.

4. General

Finally, although not exactly or specifically designed for the purpose of protection of conflict of interest, Article 58 of SEL prohibits sale, purchase and other dealings in securities using unfair measures, schemes or technics, which can be applied as a measure of preventing unfair transactions and conflict of interest, in addition to prevention of other unfair dealings, such as insider tradings.

James Riley

I'd like to start with a simpler model of looking at conflicts of interest because I don't know if any of the non-English lawyers have looked at the proposed rules by the TSA because when I get to them I would venture to say that they are not common sense rules in anybody's world. I think when you look at conflict of interests you have to look at them in two broad terms.

The first is when I'm exercising a discretion to act on behalf of someone else and I think instinctively you can come up with a series of rules that promote the fairness of that type of activity. For example, if I am dealing with you as a trader in securities and I am dealing from my own account to fill the order I should disclose that I am a principal and not buying on the market on your behalf. At best execution rule and similar rules along those lines are very easy to promote and I think if we looked at the rules in all of the jurisdictions they'd come very close.

The tougher rules to come up with and those that I think the TSA have been wrestling with, the Japanese are wrestling with, the Canadians have wrestled with and the Americans are wrestling with are those rules that you need to protect the integrity of your system, and paramount to that is insider trading because what everyone feels instinctively is that if I have information that is not generally available on the market place then I should not be able to reap the advantage of that until it has been generally disclosed. When you look at, for example, the rule in England now with respect that when you can act on recommendations or act in advance of the publications recommendations you see tension between two rules. There is a concept that it is like insider trading, its unfair that if I have created this information that I should be able to act on it before everyone else knows about it. One example is the criticism that Solomon Brothers took a few years ago when they were taking positions in the bond market in advance of pronouncements of which way interest rates were going to go generally. On the other side of that is the tension that comes from wanting the experts in the market place to come up with research to get the benefit of their work product either directly by trading for their own account or indirectly trading for their particular clients. I think I'd like to see the first Friday afternoon when everyone sits around and figures out how many shares you need to fill your order for the next Monday.

This brings me to the problem which I think the English rules will create in spades and that is they are going to be incredibly hard to enforce. I think that if you take a rule that has one general proposition and then 14 exceptions and try to explain that to someone that is on the trading floor you are inviting disaster one way or the other. Either there will be no trading in that position or there will be complete, flagrant abuse of the rule when they say: 'well, I thought I had to fill these orders and that I thought it was reasonable and fair' and all of those things that go into those rules. The poor compliance officer is going to have an impossible job trying to come up with a set of rules that will help the traders understand what they can do and, indeed, I think will be a very unpopular individual when viewed from the trading prospective.

All of those things are prospective, I think in the long run all of the rules will shake themselves out but I think that the rules which will cause the most problems are those ones that go towards protecting the integrity of the system and where there is a tension between the clear profit motive and wanting to make sure that generally you want to be seen dealing fairly with people.

In Ontario, and I'm speaking particularly for Ontario and not the rest of Canada but which is the focal point for changes right now, through actions taken at the federal level basically all other financial institutions other than broker dealers can now own investment dealers, broker dealers or anyone who is in the securities business so that means that banks, trust companies and insurance companies can now own investment dealers. By and large most of the activity has taken place with the banks taking interest in securities dealers or starting up their own new operations. Paralleling the changes at the federal level which acted to let people own securities dealers were changes which were designed to encourage proper disclosure of potential conflicts of interest and they run through a whole gamut of securities dealings, but the highlight of the rules is when you have a bank whose wholly-owned securities dealer is underwriting dealings of a banks customer and there are extensive rules which are designed to ensure that if the money is being used to repay loans that are outstanding to that bank that they are disclosed, that the general status of compliance with the loan convenants, status of the security and all of those things which I think will make it very hard for a securities dealer to take an issue to market if it is clear that the bank is trying to take an advantage and shift what would otherwise be a bad loan from its books onto the public's books.

The Toronto Stock Exchange is coming out with conflicts of interest rules, although those rules I think even today have not been drafted yet because they are looking at several models and trying to decide what additional rules they need in addition to their existing rules like best execution and disclose of whether you are trading as principal or agent.

Banking authorities have done very little in this area so far, except to ask each of the banks to come up with a conflicts of interests policy. I think there is a little unfairness in that in the sense that Canada does not have an extensive history of formal Chinese Walls that are vetted by regulators and maybe even subject to litigation so that I think that it will take some time for the Canadians to come up with effective Chinese Walls. Those Chinese Walls are the walls that relate to the commercial bank and the securities dealing banks at the same time Ontario has changed its insider trading rules, from rules that had a defence if you did not make use of your insider information in connection with your trade which effectively meant that you had to prove that the person who had the information maybe didn't trade on it, maybe there was a restricted list.

In order to establish that you didn't make use of defence now you will have also have to prove that you had appropriate procedures in place which everyone is interpreting as Chinese Walls. Again there is no indication as to what will be sufficient in order to create your defence so I think there may be some very interesting litigation coming up in the next few years.

The last point that I have to make is on the unfortunate position that the Japanese and the Americans find themselves in vis-à-vis Canada right now, because Canada has effectively deregulated its securities market which I think was perceived as good by most Americans, but has effectively put an requirement in place that before you can come into Canada you have to prove that there is reciprocal treatment in your home jurisdiction for a bank or a securities dealer that wants to get into the bank or securities dealing business, in the United States or Japan for example. Thus far, in Canada there has only been one American house let in, I suspect there will be one more, there might be a Japanese house let in and there is one English house that has been let in. The irony of it is that I think that the American rules and the Japanese rules are designed to try and protect conflicts of interests. I think they may have become more, in the last few years, spurs to competition for other reasons but I think the small irony of it is that the door is now open but what is keeping you out is your conflicts of interest rules.

Simon macLachlan

Are you saying that in Canada a bank may own a brokerage company?

Answer

Yes.

Simon macLachlan

And if that happens and the brokerage company is promoting an issue, if part of the proceeds of that issue go to repay the bank - full disclosure of that is required?

James Riley

Yes, the rules are quite precise as to what you have to disclose and effectively will make it very clear that if the money is being used to repay what is essentially a bad debt then that is what you have to say.

Simon macLachlan

In this country, if BZW is promoting an issue and some of the proceeds are used to repay Barclays there wouldn't be any disclosure, would there?

John Robertson

No.

Simon macLachlan

What about the United States?

Joni Nelson

Well certainly in the United States you have to disclose it. In the United States if you are selling securities you have to say the what proceeds are for - if they are going to pay off shareholders, founding shareholders, loans. But I can't believe in this country that there is not some other rule that would require you to disclose.

Simon macLachlan

Well you'd have to disclose where the proceeds were going to repay bank borrowing but I don't think you'd have to say those happen to include borrowings from Barclays Bank which happens to be the parent of BZW.

Joni Nelson

Even under the general fraud disclosure rules of the United Kingdom, forget the Securities Act?

Answer

I have to confess, I haven't actually been confronted with this type of situation. I would have thought with all the expert lawyers here that they would be able to answer that question for us.

James Riley

Would you also have to disclose if the bank had been, for example, the one that had insisted that the transaction be done? You have potential conflict in that you have to get consent from the client and from both broking and commercial banking sides.

Joni Nelson

Yes, that is the conflict that I was referring to, that you have a situation where one set of rules requires you not to share information and another set of rules such as Fraudulent Conveyance Laws and Bankruptcy Laws of the United States absolutely insist that you do. You are deemed to know on both sides.

Michael Robinson

I wonder Jim if you would please add to your comments the requirement of the ongoing statements of potential conflicts to clients generally.

James Riley

There are actually two areas which I think are worth getting in to on that line.

At the Ontario Securities Commission level part of the conflicts of interest package essentially are other rules designed to give positive behaviour to the broker. The first is the creation of a standard that you must deal fairly with your customers which is derived from the so-called US shingle theory - when you hang out your shingle with your broker dealer you are supposed to deal fairly with everybody in the whole world when they come to you which means you can't churn their accounts, you can't do all of the things that the United States have said are bad things.

One other aspect is a need to give a statement of policies which I think has to be in place by 30th September, and the statement of policies will essentially be a declaration by the securities dealer as to its position with respect to dealing in those securities which are either the securities of a related issuer which is someone who is under the control of that broker dealer or is under common control of that broker dealer. So you can think of these complex financial empires that people are building.

Each dealer in Canada will have to come up with a statement policy as to whether or not it will deal in its family stock. You will also have to do that when you have a so-called connected issue which goes back to the bank customer who is going bankrupt and you are trying to underwrite the securities - you will also have to declare your position as to whether or not you like to deal in connected issuers. Supplementing that, in various times you will have ongoing compliance because with a connected issuer the focus of the rules is that during the course of a primary or secondary distribution of those securities disclosure must be made. On an ongoing basis on the primary dealing side you will have extensive disclosure every time you trade in your related issuer stock - you will have to mention in your confirmations or contract notes, that this is related issuer to you. You will have to disclose, when giving advice, whether its a related issuer and in the advice area, if you are doing a recommendation, you can't give a bigger play to someone who is a related or connected issuer as well than you give to anyone else in the same report.

All of these rules are designed to help on a disclosure basis which I happen to favour more than having a prohibition making people come clean as to their relationships. The unfortunate part of the rules, an unfortunate view not in a selfish way but in a pragmatic way, is that in their original proposals there had been a expressed course of action along the lines of rules under the Financial Services Act. That was taken out of the final rules on the basis of a constitutional argument to the extent that if private action has to be taken, it will have to be solved on a court basis, we will have to look to the US rules and we may look to analogous some Canadian case law as to whether or not when you create that kind of duty you give an implied civil right of action.

THE EFFECT OF BIG BANG ON CAPITAL RAISING AND FINANCING ACQUISITIONS

Richard Ramsay

I will discuss the effect on equity capital raising and financing of acquisitions after Big Bang. It looked at one stage as if we could expect some quite considerable changes in this area. Various securities houses were queuing up to break through their rights issue barrier to show their prowess but that has not actually happened yet. I am not sure that it won't happen and I think its quite useful to run briefly over the background before moving on to what has happened and then perhaps suggest some pointers for the future.

I think you will find that there has not been that much change as yet and I will comment on that later. So I'd now like to discuss briefly about the background, and I'll cover this under three headings. First, what's been happening in the markets both in the United Kingdom and world-wide, secondly, what has been happening amongst the competitors, and thirdly what has been happening in market psychology.

1. The Market

I think that the major point here, which I am sure you are well aware of, is that there has been a very significant increase in the internationalisation of markets. What you do in London is interesting elsewhere, what happens elsewhere is now interesting in London. Investors are looking at both their markets and other markets and they are looking at whether it is better to be in one or the other. I think separately there has also been on the corporate finance side a significant step up in the activities of companies outside their own countries. There has also been a change in regulations - though if you look at the number of new bodies that has sprung up, that is not always apparent. However, I think the most important thing is that the UK market has been opened up to a very considerable new number of competitors.

As the market has opened up it has seen a big step up in business. Just to take one statistic to give you a feel for this, if you look at the number of US companies acquired by UK institutions in 1986 it was about 216 and the value of those was some $14.3b. To the end of August this year the figure was that 140 deals had been done but the total value had gone up to $19.7b and I suspect that we will see that figure jump quite considerably by the end of the year. In the London market there has also been a very big step up in demand for equity capital. In 1985, the total demands were 3.8 billion, in 1986 the total demands were 9.3 billion and so far this year for the first three quarters the figure is 12 billion and its expected to top 20 billion by the end of the year. Now a lot of that has been privatisations and that has had some influence on this growth but there has also been a very big step up to the demands by corporations for capital. In short I think there has been this very significant change in the market.

2. Competition

There has been a very big increase in competition. The competition has come both from UK companies who have adopted an integrated approach to investment banking and from established companies wishing to expand in the United Kingdom. They have sought to bring all their activities under one roof, and from those houses which have adopted the non-integrated approach. People like Lazards who are going for continuing niches, Casenove's on the stock broking side, James Capel who have remained a stockbroker and stayed in the agency business as opposed to market-making. I think also what has been very important and what will have a continuing influence on capital raising is the overseas banks and investment houses who have come to the United Kingdom. Some of them have adopted link ups with local people, UBS have linked up with Phillips and Drew, Security Pacific are teamed up with Hoare Govett, we have seen US houses like Goldman Sachs and Salomon Brothers seeking to build their own businesses and whilst its very difficult to see who's going to be right in the long run there has been a very significant increase in competitors in the UK capital raising markets and that competitors with very large resources are prepared to fight hard for market shares.

3. Psychology

Has market psychology changed, has it changed with the clients, has it changed with the advice of the investment banks, has it changed with the investors? I think one other important point to make here is that there has been a quite significant change.

Turning first to the clients. What we have been seeing there are companies ceasing to be relationship orientated and moving more to be being transaction orientated. Relationship banking remains very important, but companies are becoming more and more transaction orientated and they are expecting more of their advisors. I think on the advisor front what we are also seeing is people prepared to commit capital much more willingly. In the past banks have always been prepared to commit capital but with competition and with some competitors with very large resources they are prepared to put these on the line to a much greater extent to win business. The UK market has been quite a lucrative one and many banks are keen to get their share of it. Now so far, we have seen banks committing their resources at a time when there is a raising market - its been up and down but basically it has been on a rising trend and so far there does not seem to have been too many losses. The recent hiccup in fund raising activities where companies which have sought to raise money by way of rights issues, or vendor placings with clawback, and have seen their shares left very heavily with the underwriters, may mean a change. We have seen some issues recently, the Thorn EMI one, the Trafalgar House one where over 90% of the issue has been left with the underwriters. We are all at the moment holding our breath on Blue Arrow - its rights issue is currently outstanding, the shares are trading at about 1/4p or so, nil paid, and if not taken up but left with the underwriters could severely damage the enthusiasm amongst investors for helping to fund acquisitions. Having said that, we have investors who have shown themselves prepared to back these clients, these banks who are raising money, and as I say so far they have been very willing to do it. Whether the recent spate of non successes on the fund raising side will change this remains to be seen. Certainly, investment committees when they make their decisions to underwrite issues now think much more carefully than they used too.

So we have had these changes in the background, we've had the market becoming international, we have had increasing competition and we have had people who are more prepared to use and to benefit from that competition. But what has really happened? I have to say so far not a lot. That really comes down to pre-emption rights. Before dealing with this aspect I would like to turn first of all to what people thought would happen.

Once Big Bang had happened in we all thought that we would see the bought deal coming and coming quite quickly for companies looking at raising finance. The attractions here were firstly the ability to raise money in a rather more competitive way, to go out and actually seek bids, to get banks to bid for the terms on which they would raise equity for companies. Secondly, they felt it gave them an opportunity to broaden their investor base. A very good example of this was the issue by Fisons which sought to raise some odd £90m from European investors. Fisons has traditionally been a company in which UK investors have predominated. In raising new finance it wanted to raise this from areas where it felt it didn't have a proper investor base. Fisons felt that Europe was such an area and it set out to try and broaden its investor base there. In fact, Fisons met with no success because it came up against the question of pre-emption rights.

There have been a number of bought deals but they have either been very small if they have been primary capital raising issues, or they have actually taken place in the secondary market where rather different considerations apply - investors here are buying shares already in existence and there are no real legal complications to doing it. In short the experience of bought deals since Big Bang has been very limited and has not developed as expected.

Let us look at the disadvantages to the company which is seeking to raise money, the first disadvantage is that the ultimate investors may well not be known. A company can have had promises from its investment banks as to where the shares are going to land up but it doesn't necessarily know they are going to go there. The promises may well fade away if the issue is found to be too tightly priced or indeed under priced and the investment bank can make money selling it to a rather different investor. But the fundamental problem which fund raising changes have come up against has been the question of pre-emption rights and while these remain in place I am not sure that we are going to see that many changes in the nature of fund raising in the United Kingdom following Big Bang.

Indeed, having said to ourselves at the start of the year that this would be the year of the bought deal its actually been the year when we have seen a whole series of record rights issues. The largest one has been by Blue Arrow, raising £837m to finance a US acquisition. The Midland Bank recently raised £700m and prior to that the British Printing and Communications Corporation raised £630m, so the rights issue as a technique is quite capable of raising very significant sums of money both successfully and quickly.

Looking at pre-emption rights, what are the attitudes that people are taking and why are they taking them? The pre-emption right is enshrined in UK company law but it can be disallowed if the shareholders so wish. The problems on pre-emption rights have revolved round the attitudes that institutions take. Institutions in this country are the major element of shareholders and they really fall into two major camps - insurance companies and pension funds. They have both taken very hard attitudes on relaxation of pre-emption rights in fund raising and I would like to explain briefly what those are and why they have taken them.

Their attitudes fall into two categories, the first concerns issues of shares for cash to non-shareholders and the second relates to issues of shares to third parties in exchange for shares or for other assets and the rules are different and both sets of institutions take slightly different rules.

Turning first to the Association of British Insurers which is the body which seeks to represent the views of the insurance companies to the investment community, it has taken a very hard line and it has said that it will oppose any resolution put to shareholders which seeks to disapply pre-emption rights in respect of more than 2.5% of the issued share capital where the issue is taking place for cash. That is to say that a company cannot, or is unlikely to get the approval of insurance company shareholders if it seeks to have a resolution put and passed which permits it to issue more that 2.5% of its existing issue share capital for cash.

The National Association of Pension Funds is rather more lenient. Its position is that it would not oppose any application to issue shares for cash for more than 5% of the issued share capital in any one year but they have a rolling limit of 12.5% over five years. This is cumulative so you could have 5% in one year, 5% in the next and then you'd be left with 2.5% for your remaining three years.

Looking at vendor placings which is a mechanism under which companies issue shares other than for cash, the institutions have a common stand. Their position is that companies can't issue more than 10% of their share capital at a discount to the mid-market price of more than 5% without giving your existing shareholders a chance to participate in the issue.

Now these various institutional positions have really meant the death of the bought deal or rather that is has not been born. The institutions feel very strongly about pre-emption rights, and their attitude stems around from two particular sources. First, they see themselves as the proprietors of the companies, they make up the bulk of the shareholders, they believe that when a company needs more money it should come to them in the first instance to raise that money. As regards arguments that money can be raised more cheaply elsewhere, they say (a) it's not been tried with us and (b) if there is a discount it's all within the family and we should be the ones who participate in it.

The second thing that flows from this question of the issue discount is that getting shares at various levels and getting them at a slight discount or possibly a greater discount can help them in their investment performance. Institutions these days have their performance very closely monitored, often on a quarterly basis, and if they can find anything that helps them stay in front of the market they will be very reluctant to give that up.

So they remain entrenched on that stand to maintain pre-emption rights and I don't see their position changing that much. There have been various attempts to go through that barrier, as I say Fisons, a company which sought its shareholders approval to issue shares abroad but came up against it. Indeed that was the issue which really brought this whole question into public debate which caused the institutions to look at their attitude which up until then has been a bit grey.

I think that notwithstanding the various developments which I have described earlier on as taking place in the market place amongst customers, amongst investment banks and in the psychology, there has not been the fundamental change in UK institutional investors attitudes that will really lead to a change. I think the institutional view will be there for a long time and I think as a result of that we will not see that many changes in the United Kingdom other than possibly in the area of costs and I think here companies can expect to see commissions for the various equity raising activities cut. We have seen in take-overs, the advent of the success related commission. There have been some cases like Guinness where perhaps there was rather too much success related commission but that, I think, is a rare example. I believe that we will see investment banks and institutions accepting fees and commissions which are more and more tied to success and on this front I think one activity which has helped a lot has been the privatisation programme. The Government has been amongst the forerunners in those seeking to cut commissions and have really been quite successful. Certainly, other large companies look to the investment banks and say if they can do it with you, why can't I? Some institutions have said that if we are going to keep pre-emption rights why do we need to keep commissions, after all it's us who are getting the shares, why pay ourselves? I come back to my point about institutions liking to stay in front of the investment performance race. I am sure they will try and keep commissions because it all helps.

I'd like to sum up by saying I think there has been the potential for change, there are a lot of people out there who would be very happy to see more change happening but with institutions taking the views they do on pre-emption rights I don't see that happening for some time. I think all we will see is a continuing squeeze on underwriting commissions and continuing rights issues which I think will, largely, be successful and well received.

Andre Newburg

On the matter of pre-emptive rights and rights offerings to shareholders, I'd always understood that at least on the Continent that one reason for the prevalent practice in financial markets was that companies traditionally, for political, fiscal and other reasons, tended to understate their earnings, their profits and that is distinguished from the United States where we tend to have just the opposite kind of problem as people are trying to drive up their price by showing higher earnings and paying higher dividends, so that where you have that kind of a circumstance of understated earnings, a rights offering to existing shareholders is a fair way of having them participate in the company. I suppose my question is whether there is that kind of political sentiment in the United Kingdom as well. I think there are accounting rules here that tend to be more objective.

Richard Ramsay

Yes, I'd like to take that point up. I can't speak for investors on the Continent because my experience is principally in the United Kingdom and here I think that the stance which companies adopt is very similar to that in the United States - they seek to ensure that their earnings are fairly stated. There has been a big debate recently on whether they haven't been overstating them particularly on things like acquisitions which is really quite a controversial area - the whole question of acquisition accounting and whether people are not successfully fooling a number of the investors for some of the time. So I think the question of the rights issue as a fair way of protecting investors against concealed profits, concealed reserves doesn't apply in this country. I think that both companies and investors like to feel and rightly do feel that profits and results are fairly stated.

Michael Robinson

I have been asked to give my Canadian viewpoint on whether we think the new regulatory regime will drive Euromarkets from the United Kingdom. May I make an aside here and add just a delicious little rumour that is circulating in financial markets in Toronto. We were told that after the Canadian Big Bang, or little pop or whatever it was on 30th June, that a certain major customer of a bank had announced that it was going to go into the securities dealing business and of course it was quite capable of doing that because it was very large and had all sorts of smart MBAs and what have you. Somebody said: okay put your money where your mouth is and buy x million dollars of this issue that we wish to distribute. The banker, the customer and the issuer will remain nameless. The banker supposedly did so several weeks ago on a bought deal basis and has every single one of those securities in his inventory - unsold. So, it will knock stuff into the trust department unless he made full disclosure thereof. Now perhaps that's an illustration that when one deregulates and lets players play on playing fields with which they are not familiar that perhaps they should go a little more slowly. One doubts that the bank is going to crash, because Canadian banks are very large having made one imprudent investment. However, in the long run one wouldn't like to think that all these people were rushing into areas they didn't understand.

I just made this short observation in answer to the particular question. We always had to over simplify the view that the Euromarkets were created because there was very little regulation, and securities markets are like water - they seek the lowest level of regulation. Martin Vile described to us earlier that there is a 500 page SIB rule book about to come out. He named five SROs, eight

RPBs, six exchanges, two clearing houses, the Bank of England, the Ministry of Trade and Industry and even offshore bodies like exchanges that will have some indirect regulatory authority by being recognised.

Now, I would hate to suggest that this might be the case but why wouldn't all the markets rush off to Luxembourg or something and forget all this regulatory complexity and potential conflict? It seems rather daunting to me to have such a level. In that vein, I would put forward one suggestion à propos what might happen in terms of regulators looking at the Euromarkets, and again it's from a Canadian perspective. If I gathered from the speakers earlier correctly, the new regime, the legal regime, casts such a broad definition of trade and securities dealing activities that Euromarkets and a Eurodeal, in respect of which there is no offer made in England and no listing in England, will still be caught and regulated because the activity in originating the deal and trading the various telexes between the syndicate members happens in London. If that is the case then what happened in this regard in Ontario might be useful to look at. The Ontario Securities Commission published an interpretive note, it had no force of law but everyone better obey it, which said: 'we will not exercise our discretion to interfere in one of these totally offshore deals providing the level of activity in putting the deal together in Canada, in Ontario, is minimal and there are appropriate provisions made to halt flow back, there is no listing in Canada and there is no offer in Canada and the anti-flow back provisions are left loose', a reference is made to the 90 day rule which we are all familiar with in the United States, but it's not a hard and fast rule. If something as simple as that could be done I would think that the perceived threat to the Euromarkets by all of this alphabet soup of regulators might be dissipated.

Richard Nettleton

I am here to talk about how Australian entrepreneurs have managed to raise as much money as they have done. Of course, I think the names of Holmes à Court, Adler, Packer, Bond, Elliott and Murdoch are household names not only in Australia but also elsewhere in the world. But let me assure you there is also the New Zealand contingent; there is Hawkins of Equitiore, Reynolds of Chase and Judge of Ariadne and I must apologise for any omissions.

There is also second board listing which I will talk about later on, but there are names you haven't even heard of yet. There are an awful lot more that I haven't heard of either.

Now how have these people managed to raise the money they have raised? The short answer is quite easily and in enormous quantities.

How have they managed to do it? I think one has to give credit first of all to the abolition of exchange controls or virtual abolition in Australia and New Zealand. The second thing, a point I have already raised, is the cult of the personality. These entrepreneurs are the pop stars of the late eighties. They are on the radio and on the television. Some of them of course inevitably play to the gallery and they certainly play to the gallery in the banks. We have got to bear in mind that the number of banks or other intermediaries prepared to lend them money, as someone mentioned earlier, has increased very substantially. I think the figure given was 16,000 players in the London market. The fact is there is an awful lot of competition amongst banks and other financial intermediaries who are desperately anxious to lend large amounts to people who are prepared to pay them really quite substantial fees. Of course, the people who lend them the money or raise the money for them are themselves paid by results, to a large extent, so they are developing, I like to think with the aid of lawyers, innovative financial structures.

Again, I have been asked: how do they raise the money? Well, in various ways - a typical lawyer's answer. Convertible issues - they come in as many varieties as Mr. Heinz's products. You have equity warrants attached to debt issue but split, so that you have the equity warrant element able to be dealt with separately.

But the other interesting thing that has happen is that those of you who are familiar with Australian financial history will be aware that the seventies in Australia was an era of project financing. Project financing is largely dead and buried in Australia and most of the minerals with them, but what has happened is that the skills that we lawyers learned in our project financing days are now being applied in assisting these entrepreneurs to raise the money they require. So you find quite often that entrepreneurs like Alan Bond will form a special purpose subsidiary for the purpose of making a take-over bid for company x and will raise up to 100% of the anticipated cost of the victim company and will do it on a limited recourse basis, the recourse of the banks being limited to the security of the shares in the victim company. How again, has he managed to do it? Well the short answer again is that he has a reputation which is that he always, at any rate in recent years, pays back his bank promptly and he also pays them quite substantial fees and the banks quite literally fall over themselves to lend him money. All has gone well so far.

Let us also think of the new entrepreneurs to whom I referred earlier. Australia has a comparatively small economy but there are about 300 companies currently listed on the second board markets in Australia. I think about 50 have subsequently been quoted on the main board. Many of them are in the gold mine industry and gold financing in its various forms and kinds has developed and is a highly specialised market. Of course the gold financing technics are slowly spilling into other industries because after all if you can raise money on gold in the ground, why can't you raise it on silver in the ground, or uranium in the ground or anything else in the ground?

One also has refinancings of various sorts and kinds, and the banks, with their very able executives desperate to earn the bonuses they think they deserve, are persuading even the most staid of companies that they must make better use of the assets by financing even the life blood of their industries. So one has quarrying companies for example selling and leasing back their quarries under somewhat complicated structures.

A VIEW FROM FOREIGN EXCHANGES

Donald Calvin

My remarks will cover four areas. First, what is happening in the stock markets around the world and why. Second, I will review how some of the different major stock markets operate. This is important in understanding what's happening but also to put into perspective problems that are faced in planning for the future and particularly the problems to be faced from a regulatory-legal standpoint. Third, I will discuss briefly some of the issues raised, and fourth I will then review some points to be borne in mind when planning for the future.

A quick review of the principal forces behind the globalisation of the stock markets point to four areas of activity which are primarily responsible for the revolution which is occurring in the structure of the stock markets.

1. Technological Development

Gordon Pepper mentioned these in his comments when he said "technology, technology, technology" is the prime cause driving the changes in the markets in the UK. Technological changes include the instant communications world-wide today; the computer technology that exists now not only in dealing rooms, but on stock exchange floors and in clearance and settlement systems. Instant information systems are literally wiring the world. The result of all this is that national boundaries are becoming less meaningful, if not meaningless, as far as technology is concerned.

2. Deregulation of Markets and Re-regulation Developments

The second is deregulation of the markets and re-regulation. This was also mentioned by Gordon Pepper when he said a key factor in the changes in the United Kingdom was the removal of the currency restrictions here. Deregulation is a trend that is playing a major part in restructuring of the markets. Political and regulatory barriers to the movement of capital and opening access to and between markets are among the key deregulatory developments. So-called local monopolies are ceasing to exist whether they are in brokerage, banking and securities dealing or whatever. Therefore, the local firms are exposed to competition they haven't seen before and at the same time the distinctions between the different financial functions begin to disappear. In Canada, there is this marvellous reference to the "Four Financial Pillars", Banking, Brokerage, Insurance and Money Management. The Four Pillars are no longer separate, distinct activities. Thus, old regulations are being replaced by new regulations which in some cases, may be more troublesome and burdensome than those which existed in the past.

3. Increased Investor Interest in Global Investing

The third factor, and this was mentioned by Richard Ramsay, is increased investor interest in global investing. That is, investors, particularly institutional investors, are increasing their investments outside the country of their domicile.

Why are they doing so? The benefits of diversification of investments and participation in the growth of other economies, other than in the home country, is a powerful investment incentive which has attracted a lot of people. If you look at the growth rates that have occurred, it is often greater outside your own national markets. To facilitate this trend there has been a growth in the multiple-listed stocks trading outside a home market. The number of companies whose shares are traded in more than one market has grown from a hundred or so to several hundred and the number continues to increase. At the same time there are new financial products, particularly financial futures and options, that may not exist in the home market but exist elsewhere.

4. Increased Competition for Financial Services

The fourth factor, and one of the most important is the increased competition for financial services. Richard Ramsay mentioned this and so did Jeffrey Knight by talking about how many foreign firms are now members of the International Stock Exchange here in London. The other factors that I have mentioned - technology, deregulation and greater investor interest - have led to increased competition both at home for the business of the local investors as well as world-wide.

So people are not safe by staying in their home country thinking "let the rest of the world change but I'll stay the same". Global competitors are competing with local firms on their home turf. As a result, most markets are no longer local. There continues to be aspects which remain local but most of these markets are becoming international. So to meet this competition financial firms of all types must have access to international markets as its just not good enough today to stay in their home local market.

With this background, let me review what is happening in four stock markets, that is: London, New York, Tokyo and Toronto. I will describe how the stock markets operate in those four areas of the world in a brief, overview way.

International Stock Exchange

We have heard some interesting comments about activities in London at the International Stock Exchange of the United Kingdom and the Republic of Ireland from Jeffrey Knight, but let me make a couple of points. Essentially, what you have in London by way of the structure of the stock market today is an off-floor dealer market with an automated quotation system, that is the SEAQ system, open to all qualified participants. As a practical matter there is no trading floor as we have heard and it is an order-driven system, that is dealers trade off the floor in response to orders, primarily from institutional customers. Efforts are being made, and succeeding to some degree, in the United Kingdom in establishing an individual investor base, but even with the recent increases in numbers of individual investors the percentage of individual investors in the United Kingdom is much smaller than it is in the United States and many other countries in Europe. What is being done in the United Kingdom is the building of an infrastructure of international participants to try and attract business to the United Kingdom. When people talk about the burdens which may be imposed by new regulations it must be considered seriously because you are in a situation in the United Kingdom where you are trying to get people to come in and conduct business, you don't have captives here who have to do business here, which is a major difference between other major markets.

New York Stock Exchange

Let me talk briefly about the New York Stock Exchange (NYSE). The NYSE is a two-way exchange auction market. It is centred on the trading floor. It operates totally differently than the London Exchange. The specialist, the market-maker on the floor of the NYSE, is the key element in the NYSE market. The specialist system makes the NYSE market unique. The NYSE specialist acts as an auctioneer in setting price quotations, as a dealer in executing orders for his own account and as a broker in executing limit price orders for others. Therefore, prices are established on the trading floor. Computer systems are used to support the floor not to replace it. In New York, the floor is the tip of a computer system that is enormous but you don't ordinarily see it. The New York Stock Exchange is the largest equity market in the United States and therefore its activity reflects the US's economic growth and world leadership. As long as those factors exist the NYSE will be an important market. Again, what makes the US stock markets - New York, Chicago, Boston and so forth - unique is the dealer or specialist activity on the floor.

By way of contrast the National Association of Securities Dealers Automated Quotation System - NASDAQ - is the <u>off</u>-floor dealer market. NASDAQ and SEAQ are similar systems. Again, these systems are as different as night and day to the NYSE when you come to the structure, regulation and oversight of these markets.

The Tokyo Stock Exchange

Historically, Tokyo has been the most insular of the major stock markets. Only a few years there were only 10 foreign companies listed on the Tokyo Stock Exchange. They now have a programme to list most of the major non-domestic companies in the world in Tokyo. As mentioned, they started with 10 foreign listings about two years ago, and the last time I heard, they had listed about 110 foreign companies. They may reach 500 foreign listings if there is sufficient local interest in these stocks.

The Tokyo Stock Exchange is an agency floor market, as contrasted to the London dealer system and the New York Stock Exchange two-way auction system. Orders are matched on the floor, by people called Saitori, who act as auctioneers but not as dealers. The way trades are executed on the trading floor in Tokyo can occur as efficiently in a computer system. The Tokyo Stock Exchange has a computer system called CORES in which all but 250 stocks are traded. Stated differently, the Tokyo Stock Exchange only trades shares of 250 companies on the trading floor of some 1,450 companies listed. The rest are traded in an automated computer trading system in the basement of the stock exchange building. Plans are underway to increase the number traded in CORES by 100 later this year so that there will only be 150 stocks traded on the floor. In other words, the Tokyo Stock Exchange could eliminate the trading floor a week from Sunday if they decided to do so and they would have an efficient, if not more efficient, trading system through the CORES system than they have on the floor and the mechanics and dynamics of the market would not change. Membership on the Tokyo Stock Exchange is a major issue in Japan, in part because of the understandable reluctance of the Japanese firms to open their monopoly and the ownership of the Tokyo Stock Exchange. If they could eliminate the floor through the CORES system you might wonder: why do people want to have a membership to have access to the floor? However, there are other benefits of membership. In summary, the Tokyo Stock Exchange is the largest in tho world today in terms of market capitalisation of the issues traded there, in terms of share volume - and soon, in my opinion, in terms of dollar volume. What this reflects in part is the Japanese position in the world as a principal exporter of capital.

Toronto Stock Exchange

The Toronto Stock Exchange is an excellent example of a local market in a relatively small economy that has gone international and is doing so successfully. The Toronto Stock Exchange is what I call a dual market. They have a traditional floor market similar to that of the New York Stock Exchange and the CATS system which is the Computer

Assistance Trading System. The CATS system has about 50% of the Toronto stocks traded in it but only accounts for about 20% of the Toronto Stock Exchange volume. The CATS system has been sold, or adapted by Tokyo, Paris, the Swiss, the Australians and is being considered by the Koreans and other markets so that tells you it is a pretty efficient system

By way of a quick summary, there are three principal ways that equity or stock trading is conducted:

(A) Two-way exchange auction market

The US exchanges are unique because the pricing occurs on exchange trading floors in a two-way auction market. Again from a regulatory standpoint that becomes very significant in how you regulate that market.

(B) Agency markets

The best example of agency markets is the Tokyo Stock Exchange. The Tokyo Stock Exchange is a floor agency market with off-floor dealer participation. There are no dealers on the Tokyo trading floor so that activity originates upstairs.

(C) Dealer markets

NASDAQ and SEAQ are examples of dealer markets where all the activity occurs upstairs. Again, an important distinction is that a broker is your agent and a dealer is your adversary. As a result the problems in regulating a dealer versus agency markets are different.

A fourth system is emerging. These are the automated off-floor execution systems where everything occurs off-floor. With such a system you can trade from anywhere in the world, anyone can be a member - and the Swiss have such a system. It's called SOFFEX. The SOFFEX system is the acronym for the Swiss Options and Financial Futures Exchange. In the view of some experts, this type of system is the wave of the future because it does everything, i.e.

executes orders, reports the completed transaction and maintains essential information about all transactions handled in the system. Since all the information is automatically entered into the system, clearance and settlement is done efficiently. SOFFEX is scheduled to begin operation in March 1988, so, for our purposes here, we only have three systems but we are going to have four in the very near future.

All these systems have benefits and all have disadvantages. None is the perfect system for all types of securities transactions.

There are common factors in all the stock markets. These are: 1. there is more competition; and 2. there is more business to be done; 3. as a result there are greater profit opportunities in these markets than you ever had before; and 4. at the same time, greater capital resources are required. Access to capital is required and that is one reason why people are amalgamating with larger firms, they have to have access to capital just to keep up. 5. All these markets reflect the different historical origins and their local cultural and social environment.

So what you need to have today - and this is the sixth and last common factor - is the ability to operate multi-nationally, as contrasted to operating locally.

There are several issues which this discussion raises: will there be one world-wide equity trading system? Who will control the system or systems? Exchanges? Investment firms? Vendors? Information services? The Government? Who will be intermediaries and participants i.e. exchange members? Who will regulate and how?

There is no clear-cut answer at present to these questions.

In summing up let's take a quick look at what one might do in planning for the future. Whether you are approaching planning for the future from the standpoint of broker, dealer or institution, an exchange, a lawyer or solicitor advising clients, or an issuer, there are certain factors that you might bear in mind when you look at what you must do in response to these developments.

One is recognise the importance of flexibility - when you are in a revolution you have to be flexible, you don't know who your friends or enemies are and here you don't know what will happen next so you don't want to invest all of your resources or your activity in one direction. At the same time you need to be adaptable because there is a tendency today for very rapid change as contrasted to what happened in the financial industry for years where you had an emerging trend over a period of years. Now it's very rapid, now a new product can replace an old product overnight, a new system can oust an old system overnight and so forth.

What is terribly important is people, because the one advantage that one firm can have over another is not only the competence of its people but their relationships and their qualifications and their dedication - factors which are important in today's world and particularly in many new firms where they have qualified people but they may lack dedication to the goals of their firm.

There is the need to take a longer view. If you take a short-term view and don't make a profit a week from Sunday and you get out of the activity you may expend all your capital before you really find out what is happening. So you need to take a longer view, study the problem, make a decision and stay with it and succeed over the long pull.

You need to be innovative with all these changes occurring. If you are innovative and develop a new product or new system, or whatever, that may give you an edge over your competitors.

At the same time you need to maximise your resources because to everyone, no matter how much capital resources one may have, resources are still limited and therefore team work and planning become important.

Finally, and probably the most important and difficult part, are the regulatory and legal aspects because we are operating on a world stage today where the game is being played while the rules are being written.

Al Sommer

Let me paint a picture a long way in to the future. First of all I start with the proposition that technology will always win. Technology is retarded by laws, by prejudices, by vested interests, but eventually it will win. Now in 1973, just after I went on the commission I had a demonstration with all the other commissioners of the so-called "black box market". Now, I am going to give you an image of what the "black box market" as a world market would look like. You are the portfolio manager of a large institutional investor, somebody has given you a personal identification number, a PIN, you punch in the PIN on your computer and you want to buy a 100,000 shares of GM, Toyota, Hanson whatever it is some place, you don't really care what market its executed in, but you punch that in and the computer sweeps the markets of the world to finds out who is a seller and in what quantities and at what price. The computer picks out, if its a million shares lets say it picks out 500,000 shares in Tokyo, 300,000 shares in Hong Kong and maybe 200,000 shares in Buenos Aires, executes it through the computer, transfers that stock from a central depository or on the books or however the system develops, so that you are now credited some place with a million shares of this security and your account is debited with whatever the price of it was plus the cost of execution. The technology for that is here today, it is in existence today - that could be constructed technologically. Why isn't it done? Cost is a consideration but a far more important cost are the national boundaries of the systems we have in place with regard to requirements of disclosure, limitations of listings of securities, all those things and I would say to you, those of you who live another 50 years and are here today, will come back and say: by God, Al Sommer was right - that's what we have got.

Leigh Masel

I'd just wanted to say something about the Australian market, mainly because its not covered by Don's overview. If you really didn't want to travel the 26 hours by plane from London to Sydney or the 30 hours to get to Melbourne, assuming you would stop in Sydney for an hour, the nearest replication of what is happening in Australia is Toronto. There are very marked similarities between the Australian system and the Toronto Securities Commission and the Toronto Stock Exchange.

Australia has about 5% of quoted stocks in terms of world capitalisation. Surprisingly enough that makes it number six in the world markets and it is only exceeded by the United States, the United Kingdom, Japan, Canada, Germany, Australia comes next. We have seen, in Australia, commencing on 1st April 1984 - April Fools Day, enormous structural change, we have seen all the sorts of things that have happened in other parts of the world and in fact the change in Australia preceded changes in the United Kingdom and possibly by a year in Canada. We have seen the abolition of negotiated commissions, we have seen liberalisation of entry, corporate membership, bank ownership, freeing of the Australian dollar, suspension of exchange control and non-resident participation all in the process of three years.

The biggest event in 1987 certainly has been the establishment of the ASX, the Australian Stock Exchange. As I touched on the reasons for that earlier, I won't repeat it. Suffice to say that there were two forms of competition which were really open to Australian securities dealers. Competition could be as between states and therefore the states would compete amongst themselves or more realistically, they could compete in world markets and there is a realisation that Australia is really competing in terms of worlds markets. Australians were somewhat surprised that in May 1984 when there was a very much publicised edition of Euromoney that there were some 236 corporations whose stocks were so internationally acceptable, that there was an active liquid market for them in more than one exchange. Australians were somewhat surprised to find that, out of the 236, 84 were American, 49 were Japanese, 17 were German, 16 were Australian, 13 were British, 12 were Canadian and 10 were Swedish and the rest. So Australian stocks are traded internationally in London and on NASDAQ and the formation of the Australian Stock Exchange is an indication of the competitive environment in which Australia finds itself and in which it needs to establish the same, efficient market systems which I think exist today in Toronto.

Peter Dey

There have been a number of factors mentioned leading to reform. I wanted to throw in one further and that is the need, at least domestically, for increased capital to be available to investment bankers who are competing in a bought deal environment and the restrictions upon ownership and access to the Canadian markets denied access to capital to many of the domestic dealers, and it was this need for capital that was a major factor in the reform in the Big Bang that occurred in Canada.

In addition, because we live in a provincial state there was competition amongst the jurisdictions to create the most comfortable environment for the capital markets within Canada and that competition both amongst the provinces and between the provinces and the federal government impelled Ontario, although it would never be admitted, that Ontario was anxious that it remain the centre for the capital markets in Canada. The result was a very immense reform, the dropping of virtually all restrictions against financial institutions - there are Four Pillars by the way - and the

Four Pillars have turned to dust and from an international perspective all of the restrictions against non-resident participation in the capital markets will be gone by June 1988.

This has lead to some interesting models for entry into the Canadian capital markets. There are some firms, such as Goldman, Sachs and Warburgs, who are entering directly, they are establishing modest bond trading desks at the outset with some corporate finance assistance both available domestically and from their parent firms. Firms such as American Express have invested taking a minority interest in one of Canada's leading brokerage firms and whether that will increase or stay at the level that it currently is of 30% remains to be seen.

A third model involves offshore commercial banks taking a substantial interest in investment banks such as Securities Pacific's recently announced investment in Burns-Fry in Canada and also First National Bank of Chicago's investment in Wood-Grundy. One of the issues raised by that is when one of the US commercial banks invests in a Canadian investment bank which has an investment banking operation in the United States - it runs foul of the Glass-Steagall Act and so what has happened is that the investment banking operation in the United States has to be shifted off to the local people.

There are also investments being made by Canadian commercial banks directly in Canadian investment banks.

In closing, the only other thought I have is that there is immense pressure upon the securities regulators in the major jurisdictions regulating capital markets in the world to accommodate financings and financial activity that are occurring on a global basis. This will require a dropping of some of the narrow, provincial approaches which we have all encountered in the course of trying to complete a financing on an international basis. It will require confidence by one regulator in the ability and the rules that have developed in other jurisdictions. There is a need for flexibility and I hope that regulators are worrying about the same issues that we are worrying about.

THE FUTURE

Stanislas Yassukovich

The present has turned out to be far more complicated than any of us had assumed and far more time consuming. Perhaps the cleverest aspect of the British Government's initiatives in the field of so-called deregulation was to follow very closely the well-known principle that the best gamekeepers are made from reformed poachers. Therefore, the brunt of the preparation of both the organisational structure of the new regulatory system and the nitty-gritty of devising the rules and regulations by which we will live, has in fact fallen on the practitioners through the establishment of so-called Self-Regulating Organisations and of course the Recognised Investment Exchanges, each of which in their applications to the SIB for recognition in those roles, thereby permitting practitioners to gain authorisation through membership of those organisations and in that preparation are being called upon essentially to devise the detailed rules and regulations by which we will live in future.

Since we are all blessed with an excessive amount of in-house legal talent, both of the genuine and of the c-lawyer type, I suspect that we have gone far in excess of even the spirit of the Act in terms of the regulatory structure that we are now building - something which, I predict, will cause an increasing amount of concern on the part of the Government. The political pressure which led to a very intense focus on the regulatory process in the build up to the elections, punctuated as that build-up was by a number of highly-publicised City scandals, that political pressure has abated, at least for a period of five years, and the authorities will now begin to focus much more on whether the monster that has been created does in fact achieve its objective of developing a method of investor protection which is appropriate in the light of the new and globalised markets, and whether it does in fact enhance the potential of the City of London to take its rightful place as the premier financial centre in this time zone, or whether on the contrary, so many cracks open up that the level of investor protection is not as high as originally assumed and whether that same complexity, as it affects the wholesale markets, does not drive a certain amount of activity now centred in London off shore to other centres in this time zone that are far less advanced in their process.

There are a number of paradoxes that are emerging in terms of the regulatory process. There was initially the 'sledge hammer to crack a nut' aspect because, of course, the overwhelming majority of activities in the financial services area and in the securities area, in particular in the City of London, are of a wholesale nature dealing with knowledgable and sophisticated investors, namely institutions. An equally significant proportion of the total activity is essentially entrepôt business where city institutions are intermediating world capital flows which have grown very rapidly in recent years. A very small part of the activity touches the individual investor.

In fact, the individual investor remains a very small constituency despite the publicity that is being given to the growth in direct share ownership, and in fact we have recently seen statements that we now have almost as many individual shareholders as we have trade union members in this country - there is only a gap of a couple of million between the two numbers. The facts are that, although according to the latest survey carried out jointly by the Stock Exchange and the Treasury, there are some nine million adults who directly own shares, some 50% of that total number actually only own a single share which will be either a share in the business in which they are employed or will be one of the recent privatisations, probably TSB, British Telecom or British Gas. This leaves roughly only four and a half million people who would have, what we would term, a normal investment portfolio, a balance of different equities which they own directly, as opposed to membership in a pension fund or beneficiaries under life insurance schemes. So we are really talking about a very small constituency and that hard core four and a half million people I would submit is a somewhat expanded, fairly stable number that has always been there and tends to be the more sophisticated members of the community rather than representing brand new shareholders in need of an extraordinary amount of protection.

One of the paradoxes is that the intermediary community that has at the moment the best mode of access to individual investors namely the clearing banks and the building societies who operate vast networks of physical branches on the high street, that community is likely to fall under the most liberal regime in terms of the Financial Services Act, in terms of code of conduct and code of business practices, in dealing with investors because that community is opting, not unreasonably, for membership of not the main stream self-regulatory organisation, the Securities Association, but IMRO which is in a sense a fringe SRO at least in terms of being outside the main stream of securities business in the City. IMRO is able not to implement all of the assumed investor protection devices which TSA, dealing with a far more complex range of activities, is going to have to implement. For example, the concept that an individual dealing with a potential investor must himself or herself somehow be an authorised person working obviously for an authorised business which must have some official registration, must have some qualification similar to the registered representative system that exists in the United States. That concept will not be implemented by IMRO on the grounds that a branch office manager dealing with a potential investor is merely transmitting an order to purchase or sell securities to a central office somewhere in the organisation where that order will actually be transacted. In fact it has always been a fundamental principle of investor protection regulation in the United States that individuals dealing directly with the public must themselves be individually within the regulatory framework as registered representatives. That, in fact, will not happen here, so that seems to me one of the first paradoxes, whereas, the professional trader who is dealing in securities with professional counterparties, primarily sophisticated institutions or indeed other market-makers, will in fact, have to be a registered person under the rules of the Securities Association. So the Prudential, you could argue, will end up having a higher degree of investor protection than the famous Aunt Agatha in Brighton, which seems to me to be one of the basic paradoxes.

I think another obvious lapse in the system which we will see attracting increased attention, and which is perhaps the last phase of reform and change of the whole process in the securities industry here, will be the new issues process. Again, coming from an American regulatory background where the emphasis is on disclosure and on investor protection particularly in new issues, in new financings which are deemed to potentially have the greatest amount of speculative danger, one has been surprised to find that the whole of the regulatory process as devised by the FSA focuses effectively on secondary market activities rather than primary market activities.

Primary market activity will continue to be the direct responsibility of the DTI who are expected and are already beginning to promulgate measures dealing with the primary market. The primary market falls outside of the responsibility of the SIB or of TSA. Obviously to some extent it falls within the preview of the Recognised Investment Exchange, but primarily, it falls outside of the terms of the Act. Indeed, even under the previous legislation that we had here, primary market activity was one of the principle focuses - the Prevention of Fraud of Investments Act, which was the main legislative code that we operated on prior to the FSA, emphasised very much, primitive, perhaps by today's standards but nevertheless fairly detailed regulations governing the issuance of a prospectus in connection with a new offering.

It's also amusing to note that the various Parliamentary Acts passed to facilitate each large privatisation issue, in every case, exempted the Government as the vendor from the provisions of the Prevention of Fraud of Investments Act. So that the largest new issues that had been undertaken and those that have been primarily focused to the public have essentially sought to involve, for the first time, the public in a broad way in the securities investment industry were carried out exempted from the past, or existing at the time, regulatory structure designed to achieve a certain amount of investor protection. The Act itself which actually replaces the PFI does not focus on the whole issue of investor protection in the case of new issues. We have seen the very largest issues essentially being distributed through the media, through a heavy reliance on media advertising, particularly television advertising, which obviously involves a relatively selected presentation of the critical facts with regard to a new issue.

I think that obvious gap will have to be closed and that either the new issue process will be incorporated somehow within the structure that is being developed, or there will be a far greater emphasis in the directives coming from the DTI on such matters that are second nature to those of us who were brought up in the US environment, such as the appropriateness of an investment to a particular individual in the light of his financial circumstances such as full and fair disclosure and so on because that is, it seems to me, a gaping hole at the moment.

So much about the peculiarities of the present situation. I was asked essentially to speculate on the future and I will try and do that in two parts. First focusing on London and the United Kingdom, both in the domestic prospective and the international perspective. Clearly the reforms that have been carried out in the lead up to Big Bang and in consequence of Big Bang and in consequence of the deregulatory atmosphere created by the political environment, those consequences are vast and we have not yet seen the game fully played out. As in the United States after the first much more limited deregulatory steps were taken, essentially focusing on eliminating the monopoly power of the stock exchange there through the elimination of fixed commissions, as in Wall Street we saw the economic consequences on the structure of the financial community played out in two fairly distinct phases so we will see also a second phase of consolidation, mergers, de-mergers, reshuffles, reconglomerations, deconglomerations in the financial community in London affecting all, I suspect, of the principle sectors - everything from high street banking or consumer financial services to the whole sale markets, to the securities markets, to the corporate finance activity. The starting gun to the second phase, I would submit, has already been fired - I think the abortive negotiations between the Union Bank of Switzerland and Hill Samuel, one of our principle accepting houses here, represents that starting gun. All basically generated by the strategic reality which is summed up in the expression: 'big is beautiful and small is sweet'. In other words, clearly as in so many other areas of economic activity, as in so many other industries and commercial enterprises, it's becoming clear that in the globalised markets one either has to operate at the global scale or one has to find a niche, be it geographic or be it functional, one must at all costs avoid the middle ground, the great swamp in between where one is too small to be truly global or to be competitive on a global scale and yet too big to be economically successful as a niche operator. A great many London-based institutions still find themselves in that middle swamp and they will have to extricate themselves either by joining up with others to operate and compete at the global level or by altering their business, their strategies by ridding themselves of unwanted activities in order to focus as a niche player in a particular speciality. As that process develops there are quite legitimate fears that the indigenous share of the total community will be reduced below whatever level is deemed to be an appropriate level from a national interest point of view and there clearly are fears that that will happen and that the community of London will be caught as the meat in a North American/Japanese sandwich and that there will be far too few survivors, particularly in that category that seek to operate on a global scale. It will be that fear, of course, which prompts further consolidations in the hopes that there can be created two, three, whatever the market can stand, players who can be credible competitors on a global scale. The simple definition of what it takes now to be competitive in the global market is a very simple one, one must have a full scale and substantial presence in each of the three time zones - North America, Europe and the Far East. Many have such a presence in two but not in all three, relatively few are already positioned to develop in all three and the next phase of consolidation and reshuffle in the City will throw up perhaps two or three, I doubt that it will be more than that, purely indigenous UK-owned firms that are credible competitors on a global scale.

The next phase will also, as I have already suggested, be one of review of the consequences of the Financial Services Act and of the structure. That review will be prompted by an evolution which I think is fundamental to the whole process that we see on a world-wide basis and which is not just confined to this market. That is the following potential conflict that has been a consequence of this very dramatic and rapid revolution in information technology. Those of us who are in the securities business, or whose financial activity is focused primarily on the securities area have been, of course, benefiting from the trend towards disintermediation. Financial assets that were previously static, if you like, and in the hands of deposit collecting institutions have been very rapidly securitised through a process that has disintermediated that particular type of intermediary - the intermediary between the classical saver and the user of capital. The commercial bank has been, in a sense, the victim of the technological process of disintermediation and securitisation.

I think the next phase is that those who are operating in the business of information technology as a prime business will begin to disintermediate the classic market-makers in securities. We see signs of this already as there develops a grey area between the so-called financial information and quotation or price vendors, those who operate world-wide systems for distributing electronically financial information, and those who are still, in theory, the origin of that financial information in particular prices, the market-makers. As that grey area develops one will begin to see a certain process of disintermediation of the classic market-making function because the classical market-making function will be in fact be substituted by a greater communication facility between end users and buyers and sellers of securities. That process in itself will tend to accentuate one of the major problems associated with the globalisation of financial markets and that is the still very marked lack of any harmonisation of securities regulation even between major centres not to speak of the some of the emerging centres. That conflict will, I think, be a particularly vivid example or striking pointer to what I consider to be the major dilemma that will mark and totally overshadow the future development of the securities industry post Big Bang London and all the other mini bangs that are taking place in so many other centres. That is the simple fact.The impact of information technology and the globalisation of financial activity that is a result takes place against an environment that is still largely national in terms of regulatory system. It also takes place within a corporate environment and in an environment of corporate law, if you like, that is still essentially national and domestic. That is producing a growing conflict which one sees in a number of areas. In a regulatory area we will see it more and more, as capital flows accelerate, as the velocity of movement of capital accelerates and as there develop further conflicts between market practices and market traditions in various centres with investors using those centres within the same 24 hour time span on a regular basis through 24 hour trading. The transparency and the integrity of prices quoted in one centre are clearly already very different from those in other centres and yet the same investors within the same day will be very often be turning positions on a 24 hour basis having taken a position in Tokyo, turned it in London and then again in New York later in that 24 hour period.

Increasingly there will be frustration and complaint on the part of a globalising investor community at the disparity between regulatory practices, between customs, between the levels of price integrity that exist in various centres. This will tend to focus further attention on the part of national authorities and the harmonising process, of course, will be a levelling up, if you like, and not a levelling down so that centres that are now relatively loosely regulated will become more regulated. We will therefore see on an international scale an example of what we have seen already here in the United Kingdom that the widely used expression 'deregulation', of course, is grossly misleading and a perfect example of misleading information is in a prospectus because deregulation here has actually meant more regulation and deregulation globally will mean more regulation within various centres who are joined in the global process but are clearly way behind in terms of state of the art regulation. So they are all busily reading the Financial Services Act and they will all be busily reading the rule book produced by the TSA and their draftsmen are already at work on imitations of those articles, I am sure. So that I think will be one major factor that we contend with in the future.

The other example of the, if you like, dicotomy or the contrast between the reality of the globalisation of financial markets and the increased velocity of capital movement is the impact that will have on corporate strategy and on the concept of corporate ownership and what corporate ownership really means, what it means to the management of those corporate entities and what it means to the shareholder constituencies. One of the underlying trends which seems irreversible despite tremendous goverment efforts in the contrary direction, at least in Europe, is that the individual shareholder is an endangered species in fact. Something, which I personally believe, carries great dangers. In fact one could say with some certainty that one of the reasons why the capitalist system in the United States has been so easily preserved even through very dramatic cycles of economic health and why it has been essentially a system enjoying political consensus for so long has been because of the high level of direct individual participation in that system through direct share ownership. As direct share ownership recedes and the individual's participation in the system is expressed through collectivised investment vehicles, be they pension funds, unit trusts, mutual funds etc. we move inexorably towards a sort of corporate state where financial power becomes increasingly concentrated in the hands of professional fund managers and where the individual feels increasingly divorced from the process which I think has very dangerous implications for the general acceptance of the system. In countries in Europe, where the privatisation programmes are moving ahead so far with great success and enjoying an enthusiastic reception the penny will drop at some point in the future that the re-creation of a private sector, the handing of industry back to the people, so to speak, from the heavy hand of government all sounds very well but if the heavy hand of government is replaced by the heavy hand of highly concentrated institutional ownership, the individual at the end of the line may not feel that his position has improved. On the contrary, he at least was able to vote the heavy hand of government out, usually getting another heavy hand in its place, but he is not in the same position to vote out of office pension fund trustees or insurance company fund managers. So there will be an increase in tension as a result but the impact on the corporation will be even greater in that the corporation will find that its own ownership constituency becomes dangerously concentrated and freedom of manoeuvre of professional management becomes limited and the independence of corporate management becomes even more threatened.

One of the ways that corporate management will seek to escape that process is by a far more conscious effort to broaden shareholders geographically as well as between individual and institutions. In fact since the scope for broadening the shareholder base within a national context will become more and more limited a UK company will not be able to escape being 85% owned by six or seven institutions. In order to escape that concentration of ownership there will be a tendency to extend ownership abroad, there will be increased pressure to reform the pre-emption rights system in this country, so that corporations become global not only in their business, as many are, but also in their form of ownership. I think that will be a healthy process but it will raise a number of issues relating to sovereignty, relating to the relationship between a sovereign state and the economic interests within that sovereign state. It will lead to increased problems in terms of the conflict between environmental and other issues that are perceived entirely on a national basis and the economic interests of a much broader shareholder constituency which goes beyond the national jurisdiction where those issues are debated. So we will continue to see that as a very clear cut example of the tensions created by the fact that financial activity is globalising rapidly, it was Walter Wriston, I think, who made the remark that information and money have always been essentially interchangeable commodities and that the history of information technology evolution is the history of financial evolution. That will become even more clear as the pace of the information technology revolution gathers and impact on financial activity still operating against the background of the traditional sovereign states world system will throw up more and more conflicts and more and more tensions which the financial community will be hard pressed to deal with on its own. Therefore, I think one of its salvations will have to be the establishment of rather better relationships than it has enjoyed in the past with government, with the industry that it serves, with the public directly, with the other professions and so on and that I think will be the main task for the financial community not only in the City but world-wide.